Upstairs in the Garden

Upstairs in the Garden

Poems Selected and New

1 9 6 8 — 1 9 8 8

ROBIN MORGAN

W · W · Norton & Company

New York   London

Some of these poems have appeared in

*The Activist, Amazon Quarterly, American Poetry Review, The
American Voice, The Antioch Review, The Atlantic, Calyx, Caprice,
Chuomo Uri, The Common Woman, Feminist Art Journal, Feminist
Studies, Kalliope, Maenad, Motive, Moving Out, Ms., The New
England Review, Off Our Backs, Poetry Northwest, Rat, The Sewanee
Review, The Second Wave, Sojourner, Sunbury, 13th Moon, The
University of Kansas City Review, Up From Under, The Voice of
Women, Woman of Power, Woman/Poet, Woman's World, The
Women's Review of Books,* and *The Yale Review.*

Since this page cannot legibly accommodate all the copyright notices,
page 245 constitutes an extension of the copyright page.

The text of this book is composed in 10.5/12.5 Avanta,
with display type set in Corvinus Medium.
Composition and manufacturing
by The Haddon Craftsmen, Inc.
Book and ornament design by Margaret M. Wagner.

First Edition

Library of Congress Cataloging-in-Publication Data

Morgan, Robin.
    Upstairs in the garden : poems selected and new, 1968–1988 / by
Robin Morgan.
    p.   cm.
    I. Title.
PS3563.087148U6   1990
811'.54—dc20   89-39137

ISBN 0-393-02832-1

W. W. Norton & Company, Inc.
500 Fifth Avenue, New York, N. Y. 10110
W. W. Norton & Company Ltd.
37 Great Russell Street, London WC1B 3NU
1 2 3 4 5 6 7 8 9 0

For Marilyn Joy Waring

Contents

CONTENTS

1 0

CONTENTS

1 2

Foreword

Upstairs in the Garden contains work selected from four previously published books of poetry, as well as a substantial section of new, hitherto uncollected, poems. Choosing what to include from a body of poetry written over a period spanning twenty years was a difficult, sometimes arbitrary, task. Certain poems stand the test of time better than others. There are poems that surprise by their capacity to mature in meaning parallel with the poet's growth or, contrarily, poems which earn attention because they reveal how drastically one has changed since writing them, or even because they expose how much one knew when one didn't know that one knew it. There are poems that are cherished because the craft "played well" in them, and others—perhaps more rough-hewn—which nonetheless claim a place because they bore the message of a particular insight, a turning point.

Some of the poems included here were chosen because they have come to have a life quite independent of their maker and simply would not be excluded. "The Invisible Woman," "Quotations from Charwoman Me," "Lesbian Poem," "Arraignment," "Monster," and "The Two Gretels" were taken up by other women who made the work their own: phrases, lines, stanzas, entire sections of these poems have appeared on banners, posters, buttons, T-shirts. Sections from "The Network of the Imaginary Mother" have been chanted by women religious in rituals celebrating a spirituality defiant of and transcendent to patriarchal religion. Such use of my poetry gladdens me; it affirms the origins of poetry as an art and craft which was communal, dramatic, and neither ahistorical nor apolitical.

In any retrospective, an artist finds herself bemused to alternately pity, admire, criticize, or affirm past selves and styles. Since "I disown none of my transformations," I've tried in making this selection to include representative work from different periods. So there are the so-called academic poems in traditional forms—sonnet, villanelle, elegy. There are also structures of my own invention (e.g., "Syzygy"), blank verse, free verse; now and then, as in "Death Benefits," sprung

1 3

rhythm; and in the later poems a deliberate weaving of more traditional forms in and out of looser, more colloquial structures, encompassing strict as well as slant rhyme, internal rhymes, echo rhyme. I have made no changes in the politics of the previously published poems; indeed, in a few cases, I have returned them to an original state which I had "moderated" between last draft and first publication. I have, however, made a few minor craft revisions: the poet's itch toward precision.

I owe a debt of gratitude to a number of contemporary poets who have influenced and supported my work, in person or through their own writing, or both: Louise Bogan, Babette Deutsch, and Mark Van Doren were early teachers at Columbia University. Adrienne Rich was for many years a source of sustenance, both as friend and poet, as was the late Muriel Rukeyser. Marjorie Agosin, Margaret Atwood, Ingeborg Bachmann, Elizabeth Bishop, Olga Broumas, Marilyn Hacker, June Jordan, Carolyn Kizer, Audre Lorde, Marge Piercy, Sylvia Plath, May Sarton, Alice Walker, and Yvonne, among others, have inspired and validated the best in me, as woman and as poet. Isel Rivero has challenged me by the audacious imagery in her work, both in the original Spanish and in her own translations of that work into English, French, and German. Kenneth Pitchford was the greatest influence on my poetry from my late adolescence through my late thirties; although I have adapted them to my own purposes, his standards of excellence—so evident in his own poetry—continue to serve me well, and I am grateful.

My thanks, too, to the art colony Yaddo, for the award of a residency grant during which "White Sound" was written and several of the poems in *Depth Perception* drafted, and to the Feminist Studies Collective of the University of Canterbury (Christchurch, New Zealand): there, while a Visiting Scholar in Feminist Studies, I completed the revisions for this volume.

Blake Morgan Pitchford, my friend and a presence in my poetry for two decades, has given many of these poems the benefit of his musician's ear for phrasing, in helpful criticism and unshakable support. And special thanks go to Karen Berry, for being a first audience for more than a few of these poems; to my literary agent Edite Kroll, for years of loyalty to my poetry; and to my editor Mary Cunnane, for her aid in the selection process.

I owe perhaps the greatest debt to other women, many of whom have never written or read poetry, and most of whom I have never even met, but whose lives and words (and silences) have redefined for me the word "eloquence." The question "Do you consider yourself a feminist poet, a woman poet, or a pure poet?" is still being asked, as if art ever is created out of context, as if categories inflicting some illusory purity have anything to do with the rumpled, electric, and connective mysteries of making a poem. Although I was writing poetry long before becoming a feminist, the contemporary women's movement in the United States invited me to find my own voice, to free it from the constraints of "proper" (patriarchal) subject matter. Now, the international women's movement continues to inspire ever-broadening vision, and fresh metaphors, subjects, realities, even structures. It is a good thing to be a poet and a female human being at this moment in our planet's life; to dare speak from, of, for, and to the majority of humanity—and about a new humanity. So the work in these pages—whether in the form of rallying cry, personal soliloquy, metaphysical meditation, or love poem—is unashamedly, and in the deepest sense, "political." I have women to thank for that—and for keeping me honest.

Finally, Marilyn Waring's contributions to this book are difficult to quantify: a critical yet loving eye, the gift of more than a few titles and lines that enkindled new poems, a sustained motivation in absence or presence; but perhaps most valuable of all, a refusal to acknowledge, no matter what the cost, that the work was ready until at last it was.

None of the above-mentioned good people are, however, to be held

FOREWORD

accountable for this book. That responsibility rests with me. The
poems in these pages turn out to tell, overall, a story, with a beginning,
a middle, and an end—which in turn of course becomes a new begin-
ning. The refrains that sometimes echo not only within but between
poems are quite intentional, as if a later poem were replying to an
earlier one, as if a sensibility were engaged in ongoing dialogue with its
own facets over decades. Such a lifetime process befits any living intel-
ligence, and poetry—virtually a living intelligence itself—demands
and distills that process more than any discipline I ever hope to find.

Robin Morgan
New York City
December 1989

Monster

1 9 7 2

Mistress Beauty

Strange, but this castle is not foreign to me.
I somehow know the place. I know these halls,
however grand, are where a creature prowls
in search, he claims, of beauty. I can spy
beneath his velvet cloak to where he
wears beast-hide, wherein a blond prince dwells
in turn; within the prince, whose fairness peels
away like wax, a monster, who can free
a new prince, smiling through new monster-jaws.
I shall settle my gown, arrange my lace,
and rest my ringed white hand between his paws.
Although I fear his eyes upon my face
may yet release in me hooves, fangs, and claws,
I sense my saving death in such a place.

Elegy (I)

(in memoriam Albert Camus)

After all, the dog was only stunned:
a handsome bitch gulping for air
in the road where a car had left her lying
unmangled, nipples hard with fear.
Her eyes were open, and they knew.

We dream the day's impossible brightness
but wake at night to learn fear-sweat,
an eyeless inquisitor, wheels groaning,
matted fur, chains, a fog-slick street,
someone lost just beyond awaking.

He will not turn, nor will we wake,
except to lie beneath his wheels,
believing finally that he has passed,
and taste the red in our slackened smiles—
river that widens to no sea.

Insisting death made life absurd,
one man laughed at his torturers
and sped, of course, to his obvious end
in a car loaded with picnic hampers
one invincible summer day in France.

She rose on slim forelegs and fell
back with the rest of her polished body,
nails digging at the pavement to rise
again, trot normally away.
Then the blood blossomed from her mouth.

We read the papers, espouse causes.
Some pray. Some arch in sheeted grace,

willing each membrane to the work
only entropy will enhance.
Some sit very, very still.

The resurrection of the night
each day should teach us how, at least,
eyes watch us clawing, stunned,
for the figure hidden in the mist
breathed by our own mouth's desire.

Sleepwalking dark familiar streets,
we dream the day's impossible brightness
but wake, in time, her sight, his laughter
in effigies anointed to embrace
their only sacrament, our suffering.

The Invisible Woman

The invisible woman in the asylum corridor
sees others quite clearly,
including the doctor who patiently tells her
she isn't invisible—
and pities the doctor, who must be mad
to stand there in the asylum corridor
talking and gesturing to nothing at all.

The invisible woman has great compassion.
So, after a while, she pulls on her body
like a rumpled glove, and switches on her voice
to comfort the elated doctor with words.
Better to suffer this prominence
than for the poor young doctor to learn he himself is insane.
Only the strong can know that.

Villanelle: Dachau

(Note: Shatila is a Palestinian refugee camp in Lebanon.)

Sweetly the furrows flower red
in geraniumed blood-pits, tidy and fair,
bright as the rain Shatila shed.

The birds sing summer above the head
of the granite Jew whose stone eyes stare
sweetly. The furrows, flower-red,

are neat as the signs for tourists that read
"Exit" here, "Krematorium" there,
bright as the rain Soweto shed.

In silence, visitors are led
through rusting gates of August air.
Sweetly the furrows flower. Red

are the cheeks of children, smooth, well-fed,
the tourist children with golden hair
bright as the rain El Barrio shed.

Bored, impatient, they play hide-
and-seek in the ovens, laughing where
sweetly the furrows flower red,
bright as the rain my people shed.

Mistress Vampire

That every artery your slow spine branches
is for me to prune—all play of sinew
skeletoned, eyes socketed, hips, haunches,
smile, and walnut brain decaying tissues
ripe as my fear that defoliates this midnight—
that what you are is lost to me as if
I never knew you, that even our love's sweat
dries on the skin in seconds: not for myself
I mourn, though you melt through my flesh like a bullet's silver,
sing like a splintered stake green in my heart.
I who enshroud your human shape could labor
to turn you immortal, but love that art
less than your waking, dawn-lit, alive, alone.

Why do you lie so still? What have I done?

The Summer House

Something about that face is unlikable, heavy
with still-firm cheek and pretension,
not even sensual or bored.
Too round, for one thing, like a lewd child's
or incontinent old man's face, chubby, chewing;
a petulant chin, a nose that's coarse and coy,
and pores more prominent than cheekbones.
The lips though, they seem framed
for almost saying something,
almost risking that one kiss before they close
around sleep-fetid breath.
Those eyebrows appear perpetually raised
to arch over sullen lids
cupping more than necessary of the eyes'
attempt to widen in delight at what
they'd wish to squint against in fear.
See how expressions populate that face,
easy-mannered as acquaintances invited
to summer at a country house
which will be emptied at the first slight frost.
Who could believe the owner
keeps, whole winters through,
one caretaker to tend the fire,
except for an occasional spume, a glance
like the signal for despaired-of strangers
or one untimely guest?
So I was told, at any rate,
when I was there last summer.

Quotations from Charwoman Me

You never asked to be a master
and God knows (if She would only say so)
I never asked to be a slave.
Position papers, grocery lists
rain like ticker-tape on my long-march procession
past where you cheer me on,
waving from the wistful side of—let's admit it—
barricades.

You're tired of living without any joy.
You think you're going crazy.
You need my friendship.
You're afraid to demand the right
to be afraid.
You're trying very hard.
I know that, and you can't imagine
how I wish it were enough.

I need to sleep.
I never asked for this;
you never asked.
Our twenty-five-inch son
whimpers in the night
and my breasts hurt until I wake myself
and feed him.
He never asked for anything at all.
We all want just to be a little happy.

Listen, I see an older me, alone
in some room, busy on the telephone
dialing all my terrible truths.
This thing has never let me live

as we both know I might have; yet I see
this thing can cut me down
on any street or podium tomorrow—
or just let me live, alone.

Our child looks back and forth
from your face into mine, and laughs.
You worry about us, wondering if
something within us has broken.
You hold my body as if it were glass
that will cut you.
I'd stop this if I could, believe me, my dear,
I'm dying of bitterness.
I love your forehead.
Did I ever tell you that?

Lesbian Poem

*(dedicated to those who turned immediately
from the contents page to this poem)*

THETIC:

After centuries of dissecting
Joan of Orleans
as deranged and sexually perverted
objective (naturally) historians of late
have taken to cleaning up her image.
The final indignity.

It seems, you see, there was a woman
named Haiviette,
with whom Joan lived, loved, slept,
and fought in battle,
whom scholars now say only was
"a girlhood friend"
splashing their filthy whitewash over
what must have been a bed
even Saint Catherine and Saint Brigid smiled upon.

In addition, it would appear
that Margaret Murray, a woman witchcraft scholar,
has found evidence that Joan was Wica, after all.
Did you know that The Maid is traditionally one
of the names that refers to the Coven's High Priestess?
See Murray's *The Witch-Cult in Western Europe*
for further guerrilla news.

Haiviette's name, at last, burns through their silence.
Joan's ashes flicker in our speech again.
Such bones as theirs
rattle with delight
wherever women love or lie together

on the night before
we go to war.

ANTITHETIC:

I love women as a People, yes.
And my breath, work, life (and probably
my death) are bound to women
out of that love.

Yet I have also lain in beds
with some women, yes,
for a variety of reasons—
not the least of which,
surprisingly/obviously,
was male respect.

But if there is a next time, by god,
it will not be for that,
nor will we lie on a plank
in someone's correct political platform,
nor will it be done for abstract female approval
or respect.

It will be because our minds
challenge and delight each other,
and for other qualities I cannot know yet
because they will be hers,
concrete, specific, individual,
like her name.

/ / /

You can believe it will not be because
she is Woman,
or has honeyed skin
and supple legs,
breasts like pears
and a smell of the goddamned sea.

So get off my back, Sappho.
I never liked that position,
anyway.

SYNTHETIC:

> *(to Katherine Phillips, 1631–1664, "the matchless Orinda,"*
> *the first feminist poet in English who wrote of loving women)*

Having come through three decades to where
I will not settle for less than I deserve,
will not long for the past nor compromise the present,
and insist on giving as much as I expect,
I find the personal options narrowed
to the needle of my eye.

To be loved and longed for by a woman
I merely like, but like considerably;
or to be hated by another who really hates
her own most secret desire;
these are not difficult tasks,
only intolerable.

/ / /

To watch new faces fierce
with single-minded affirmation—
of what is so complex as to have built
on one side of love the bar-scene,
to have dressed women in leather tuxedos
or gingham gowns;
but also to have built on another side of love
forty-year-long enduring pre-fad
marriages between women,
calm and wit-warm in committed dignity—
this task is not intolerable,
only difficult.

To learn to love one's woman-self
has been made to seem both
intolerable and difficult.
To learn to love another woman
in one's self *is* both, and also
worth it.

Meanwhile, she whom I rarely see these years
and I
lay once on separate twin beds
and talked about these very things
through the dark room
until dawn etched sleep across the ceiling.

We must be ignorant.
We only know we may not disappoint each other
and our two lives allow,
as one feminist cell has said,
for no more fun and games.

/ / /

There is too much at stake; besides, she *is* myself:
we must be wise.

Some of you will be content
with knowing that.

Others will have to wait, forever,
to be satisfied
by the graphic details.

Arraignment

How can
I accuse
Ted Hughes
of what the entire British and American
literary and critical establishment
has been at great lengths to deny,
without ever saying it in so many words, of course:
the murder of Sylvia Plath
?

It should be sufficient to note
the already deplorable controversy
created largely by Plath's own poems and letters
referring to the dear man's peccadillos,
but

her accusation of rape could be conceived as
metaphor,
and besides, it is permissible by law for a man to rape
his wife, in body and in mind.
It is also perfectly legal for him to brainwash her children.
It is no crime for him to malappropriate her imagery,
or even to withhold her most revealing indictments
against her jailor.
It is not illegal for him to make a mint
by becoming her posthumous editor,
and he does no offense by writing, himself, incidentally,
puerile, pretentious dribbles of verse.

Having once been so successful
at committing the perfect
marriage,

one can hardly blame Hughes for trying again.
The second, also, was a suicide,
or didn't you know?
Her name was Assia Guttman Wevil.
He never married her formally—which is no crime.
She translated poems from the Hebrew
and was afraid of losing her beauty.
She is the woman in Plath's poem "Lesbos,"
and, in time,
she chose the same method as her predecessor,
finding the oven's fumes less lethal
than their husband's love.

A Jewish mother in the most heroic sense,
she took her daughter, Shura, with her.
Otherwise, identical.
What a coincidence.
But only paranoiacs would assume
that such a curious redundancy constitutes
a one-man gynocidal movement.

Plath, for example, was clearly unbalanced
for writing such terrifying poems about Hughes.
Guttman, for instance, was obviously mad
for killing her daughter
rather than let Hughes raise the child.
And I, to be sure, am patently unstable
for thinking both women were sane as Cassandra,
or even for writing this in poetry, rather than
code.

/ / /

But I am permitted, at least, to
accuse
A. Alvarez,
George Steiner, Robert Lowell,
and the legions of critical necrophiles
of conspiracy to mourn Plath's brilliance while
patronizing her madness, diluting her rage,
burying her politics, and
aiding, abetting, rewarding
her perfectly legal executor.
This is not libelous, merely dangerous, to say.
It is also perfectly legal, you understand,
for publishers to be
men
or cowards,
or members of the same fraternity.

Myself, I have no wish to be ostentatious—merely
effective.

But then, we women change our minds a lot.
That's our prerogative.
So we might not, after all,
free Frieda and Nicholas,
and one night ring the doorbell
to enter, a covey of his girlish fans,
who then disarm him of that weapon with which he tortured us,
stuff it into his mouth, sew up his poetasting lips around it,
and blow out his brains.
Who knows?

/ / /

Meanwhile,
Hughes
has married again.

Monster

Listen. I'm really slowing dying
inside myself tonight.
And I'm not about to run down the list
of rapes and burnings and beatings and smiles
and sulks and rages and all the other crap
you've laid on women throughout your history
(we had no part in it—although god knows we tried)
together with your thick, demanding bodies laid on ours,
while your proud sweat, like liquid arrogance,
suffocated our very pores.
Not tonight.

I'm tired of listing your triumph, our oppression,
especially tonight, while two men whom I like—
one of whom I live with, father of my child, and
claim to be in life-giving, death-serious struggle with—
while you two sit at the kitchen table dancing
an ornate ritual of what you think passes for struggle
which fools nobody. Your shared oppression, grief,
and love as effeminists in a burning patriarchal world
still cannot cut through power plays of maleness.

The baby is asleep a room away. White. Male. American.
Potentially the most powerful, deadly creature
of the species.
His hair, oh pain, curls into fragrant tendrils damp
with the sweat of his summery sleep. Not yet, and on my life
if I can help it never will be "quite a man."
But just two days ago on seeing me naked for what must be
the three-thousandth time in his not-yet two years,
he suddenly thought of
the furry creature who yawns through his favorite television program;

connected that image with my genitals; laughed,
and said, "Monster."

I want a women's revolution like a lover.
I lust for it, I want so much this freedom,
this end to struggle and fear and lies
we all exhale, that I could die just
with the passionate uttering of that desire.
Just once in this my only lifetime to dance
all alone and bare on a high cliff under cypress trees
with no fear of where I place my feet.
To even glimpse what I might have been and never never
will become, had I not had to "waste my life" fighting
for what my lack of freedom keeps me from glimpsing.
Those who abhor violence refuse to admit they are already
experiencing it, committing it.
Those who lie in the arms of the "individual solution,"
the "private odyssey," the "personal growth,"
are the most conformist of all,
because to admit suffering is to begin
the creation of freedom.
Those who fear dying refuse to admit they are already dead.
Well, I am dying, suffocating from this hopelessness tonight,
from this dead weight of struggling with
even those few men I love and care less about
each day they kill me.

Do you understand? Dying. Going crazy.
Really. No poetic metaphor.
Hallucinating thin rainbow-colored nets
like cobwebs all over my skin
and dreaming more and more when I can sleep

of being killed or killing.
Sweet revolution, how I wish the female tears
rolling silently down my face this second were each a bullet,
each word I write, each character on my typewriter bullets
to kill whatever it is in men that built this empire,
colonized my very body,
then named the colony Monster.

I am one of the "man-haters," some have said.
I don't have time or patience here to say again why and how
I hate not men but what it is men do in this culture, or
how the system of sexism, power dominance, and competition
is the enemy, not people—but how men, still, created that system
and preserve it and reap concrete benefits from it.
Words and rhetoric that merely
gush from my arteries when grazed
by the razoredge of humanistic love. Enough.
I will say, however, that you, men, will have to be freed,
as well, though we women may have to kick and kill you
into freedom
since most of you will embrace death quite gladly
rather than give up your power to hold power.

Compassion for the suicidal impulse in our killers? Well,
on a plane ride once, the man across the aisle—
who was a World War Two paraplegic,
dead totally from the waist down,
wheeled in and out of the cabin—spent the whole trip avidly
devouring first newspaper sports pages
and then sports magazines,
loudly pointing out to anyone who would listen
(mostly the stewardesses) which athlete was a "real man."

/ / /

Two men in the seats directly behind me talked the whole time
about which Caribbean islands were the best for whoring, and
which color of ass was hotter and more pliant.
The stewardess smiled and served them coffee.
I gripped the arms of my seat more than once
to stop my getting up and screaming to the entire planeload
of human beings what was torturing us all—stopped because I knew
they'd take me for a crazy, an incipient
hijacker perhaps, and wrestle me down until Bellevue Hospital
could receive me at our landing in New York.
(No hijacker, I understood then, ever really wants to take
the plane. She/he wants to take the passengers' minds, to turn
them inside out, to create the revolution
35,000 feet above sea level
and land with a magical flying cadre
and, oh yes, to win.)
Stopping myself is becoming a tactical luxury,
going fast.

My hives rise more frequently, stigmata of my passion.
Someday you'll take away my baby, one way or the other.
And the man I've loved, one way or the other.
Why should that nauseate me with terror?
You've already taken me away from myself
with my only road back to go forward
into more madness, monsters, cobwebs, nausea,
in order to free you—men—from killing us, killing us.

No colonized people so isolated one from the other
for so long as women.
None cramped with compassion for the oppressor
who breathes on the next pillow each night.

/ / /

No people so old who, having, we now discover, invented
agriculture, weaving, pottery, language, cooking
with fire, and healing medicine, must now invent a revolution
so total as to destroy maleness, femaleness, death.

Oh mother, I am tired and sick.
One sister, new to this pain called feminist consciousness
for want of a scream to name it, asked me last week
"But how do you stop from going crazy?"
No way, my sister.
No way.
This is pore war, I thought once, on acid.

And you, men. Lovers, brothers, fathers, sons.
I have loved you and love you still, if for no other reason
than that you came wailing from the monster
while the monster hunched in pain to give you the power
to break her spell.
Well, we must break it ourselves, at last.
And I will speak less and less and less to you
and more and more in crazy gibberish you cannot understand:
witches' incantations, poetry, old women's mutterings,
schizophrenic code, accents, keening, firebombs,
poison, knives, bullets, and whatever else will invent
this freedom.

May my hives bloom bravely until my flesh is aflame
and burns through the cobwebs.
May we go mad together, my sisters.
May our labor agony in bringing forth this revolution
be the death of all pain.

/ / /

May we comprehend that we cannot be stopped.

May I learn how to survive until my part is finished.
May I realize that I
                am a
                monster. I am
      a
      monster.
I am a monster.

And I am proud.

Lady of
the Beasts

1 9 7 6

The City of God

(in memoriam Milena Jesenká)

> "Can one be a saint without God? That's
> the problem, in fact the only problem."
> —Albert Camus, *The Plague*

I just got up. Incredible. I just got up
and lurched downstairs to put on water for tea
and wait for it to boil.
But I am the one who is simmering
already, and my god, I just got up.

What a cosmic error,
to have decided to sit at the kitchen table
and wait for the water to boil.
Look at the cockroach egg laid precisely
in the crack between the table leaves.
Another member of the colony is crawling up one chairleg,
having heard, no doubt, about the crumbheaps
left in the tufts of the chair cushions
whenever the four-year-old passes through.
Lower-east-side ninety-five-degree Manhattan July
lies flat in the rooms, not even air enough to stir
the coy dustballs nestled in corners,
under the furniture, in the crotch of each stairstep.
No Saint Elmo's Fire here,
but filth enough to cause Saint Jerome
nine mystical orgasms.

I try looking up, away—another mistaken assumption, embodying
only the ceiling. Low anyway as the New York smog,
it chuggles cracked plaster, peeling paint,
discolorations, across my gaze.
Not to speak of the moon craters,
holes the size of my clenched fist

4 5

left there from the last time we tore down a wall.
It was to give the illusion of greater space;
time being what it is, the holes remain,
now and then belching little chunklets of plaster
or an exposed beam's offsprung splinter down,
like mini-inverted volcanoes, extinct we imagine,
reminding us of their presence
in the blank, skun face of heaven.

There are holes in the face of hell too, of course:
jagged chasms leering between the antique floorboards,
gorges which have been patched and filled so many times,
only to warp again at the slightest weight.
Cockroaches crawl amicably up through them, and lately
giant water beetles—they're a treat only Saint Francis could love.
I start to meditate on whether the downstairs cockroaches
have met their brothers upstairs, whether each has some intimation
that there are comrades near, or not.
I wonder if it would be kind
to bring one of these from the table to meet a sister by the sink,
or to transport three or four—a small collective—
to parley with the batch upstairs. But which batch?
Elitist of me to choose.

After all, there are roaches in the child's room,
reeling like science-fiction monsters
through the doll-house doors;
intellectual roaches who patrol the chessboard,
music lovers who jostle the wires and wheels of the phonograph
(which is of course unplayable and a cast-of-thousands production
to get fixed, dear Jude, patron of hopeless projects).
There are the roaches who dart insectual advances

at my sleeping body, on those memorable nights
when I bound out of bed, sweating,
to shudder them off—factual visitations
more ingenious than my nightmares.
Do these comprise the phallus of their lord, Theresa?
When I light the oven, infrequently in summer,
roaches run from all the burners
like Albigensians scurrying, singed, from the fire.
I wish their reproductive habits were as chaste.
There was one frozen to death on the lowest refrigerator shelf,
next to something left uncovered, rotting.
No wonder you hunger-struck, Ms. Weil.
There was one in a glass of wine I had stupidly left
standing for half an hour, floating feet up
like a happy, dead Li Po.
There was an egg-sac affixed to a sheaf of my poems yesterday.
Meanwhile, my frenzied spraying merely
mutates their species, poisons our lungs.

Not that I want to be obsessed with roaches.
They are, after all, only one familiar symptom
of the malaise I sicken and die of, this one-dimensional
city summer of 1973, everything flat as a bad painting.
The money-worries, for instance,
which make me feel that poor, desperate Iscariot
was royally had.
Or the door on the downstairs cabinet
that falls on your foot when you unforgettingly swing it open,
or the clutter of errands undone:
shoes that need gluing, the faucet oozing
rust over an intrepidly stained tub, the grit on the windowsills,
the windowframes that stick and slant

like a Dr. Caligari set or a vision of Saint Dymphna's.
Small comfort, that I vow the next time anyone pontificates
a correct line on poverty and privilege to me
they will get smashed on their downwardly mobile nose.

What *about* the windows, the panes themselves,
given up on, given over to dirt,
all but opaque with grime, except where streaked
by pigeon crap, or my small son's hieroglyphic alphabet?
What good would it do to wash them and look through?
I have been there, I know what is there:
the whores shaking like saplings under a winter wind
in the blast of July, for a fix?
The pimps modeling patent leather and white linen?
The human shit on the sidewalk, pillowing the drunk
who speaks his dreams aloud in gape-mouthed mumbles?

Last week, in the bus, I was preoccupied with feet.
So many were in sandals, almost squinting
at a light they rarely see.
One woman's toes, grotesque contortions cramped beneath
a brave façade of purple polish—
I missed my stop, with staring.
Who could heal such feet?

Not to speak of Mao Tse-tung's alarm
that Watergate is hurting Nixon's reputation.
Or of my ill and aging mother now having to pay
the interest of her last years caring for a husband,
a terminal cancer patient, and a cranky obnoxious old prick,
even when well. Smile
enigmatically at that, Saint Anne.

/ / /

France tested a brand-new nuclear "device" last week,
drought bloats the sub-Sahara,
and Indian Untouchables are being massacred anew
for their salvation.

Where do I begin, this time?
To break the inertia, find the motor, churn the woman
and the man and even the child into cheerful and frenetic action?
And if, again,
we pacified the bruised cables,
patched up the holes in roof and floor,
whirled like dervishes in a holy
delirium of paint, wax, polish, soap, spray,
and took to the shoemakers, the cleaners, the repairshop
and then picked up from the shoemakers, cleaners, repairshop,
Martha, what then? Give me some helpful hints
on what revolutionary cleaning agent
could make the women on the corner break into bloom again,
rinse the bum's mouth with rosewater,
straighten and anoint those gnarled, nailpolished claws?
What can dust off my mother's life
or scrub the air shiny again?
How many locusts would feed the sub-Saharans?
What can scour the old men and teach the new ones
to pick up after themselves?
What scarf is large enough, Veronica, to take the imprint
of so many Untouched faces?
What can recycle them?

Not to speak of having contempt for my own self-pity,
drawn into the Cabrini whirlpool of others' pain.

/ / /

4 9

Not to speak of being detested or trumpeted politically,
but not understood.

Not to speak.

I have utterly lost the energy they sing at me about.
My energy, my energy, how I give it to them in waves, rays,
bursts, like sunlight. Hallelujah, how they bask in it.
The sun is dying, they forget, a star in some addict's blind eye
rapidly burning itself out.
What should I fix up this time, and watch decay?

The water is almost boiling.
I can't believe it, I just got up.
Already my ribcage is cast in bronze,
the congestion in my chest literal, as if
I had swallowed a lump of sponge.
The exterminator is due around noon, but it's early yet.
The house is waking into morning sounds, tightening around me.
Doors slamming open, bureaus yawning their drawer jaws in protest,
a toilet flushing more waste toward the rivers.
A man's footsteps overhead,
a small boy's voice, complaining.
Maria, deposed and co-opted, look how my child
is growing to schools which will rob him
of whatever grace and curiosity he still wears
like the nimbus encircling your blissful infant Horus
plumped on his momma Isis' lap.

And what word could descend
to melt the silence between this man with whom I live
and me, this woman half-alive?

/ / /

What blessing for his pain? No usual struggle-phase, this—
he who has also spotted god as an immense green mantis
rotating eyes unseeing over what it reaches for, uncaring.
What miracle?

The water has boiled and will crack the pot
if I don't turn it off.

Politics is not enough.
Poetry is not enough.
Nothing is not enough.

If I could smash the carapace.

Only God would be enough, and She
is constricted inside my torture-chamber ribs,
this whole planet one bubble that floats briefly
from her drowning mouth
up toward breaking.

Oh my God, if I could wholly love Thee,
wholly be Mine own, then I would not be snared
in loving all these fragments of Thee.
Let it be done, once, complete, total.
Look at Thy doorstep, Mother, Thy feet,
where I lie in all my pieces.
See the fear that streams from my bladder.
My own divinity asphyxiates within me.

Let me take myself by force, yes Heaven,
or by pity or even by patience.
But let me not remain diasporic to myself,

shards, mosaics, clues, riddles, fossils
all my loves, creations, fears, failures, triumphs.

Peel back, universe, to the slum of your meaning.
Let me recognize one other like me in the drains.
Mother, ah,
let me sleep in the buzzing breath
of Thy preoccupied embrace.

Portrait of the Artist as
Two Young Women

(for Patricia Mainardi)

Old hands,
both of us,
at consciousness-raising sessions,
at organizing, and at our respective crafts,
and old acquaintances—
we've both returned,
not having really left, to this:

You paint my portrait
while I sit for you,
writing a poem in my head
about your painting me writing.

Old hands, both of us,
we cannot help but try
to raise each other's consciousness,
reorganize each other.

You care for the pigments themselves.
Your glance quickens the practiced brush,
streaking my eyes and hair
in umbers and siennas, both raw and burnt.
You mix my face
with ochre, cadmium red and orange,
titanium white.
Daylight is clarified
by lemon yellow strontium,
the floorplanks scoured with ivory black.

I care for the words themselves:
alizarin, viridian, cobalt.
I turn "cerulean" over in my mouth,

curling my tongue around it;
I roll it along my teeth, surreptitiously,
like a sourball.
Our methods impede each other.
You ask me to sit still.

We rest—only to compare
our miseries
as artists, women, feminists.
The world misunderstands us.
We two misunderstand this much,
at least, about each other.

Raised consciousness requires of us
we use the using usefully,
but art demands of us
we use the using for the use itself.

A communication thin
as ink or linseed oil
has filtered, tentative, actual,
between our veins.
Translation would have been
in such a different shade or language
had both or either of us been
women but not feminists,
feminists but not artists,
artists but not women.

As it is, even our different sets of tools
recognize each other better than we do:
the rhythm of shape, the color of a vowel,

a verb's perspective,
the Manichean values of chiaroscuro,
the adjectival danger in a composition.

The making understands itself
more than the makers do.
It has a higher consciousness,
is better organized,
and freer than you or I
shall ever be—
except in those brave moments
when we become it,
even at the price of being doomed
to blur away afterward
like the autumn light—
vividness draining from us
as from rinsed brushes;
our own selves blank, but for that visitation's jottings,
as pages in a notebook laid aside.

Meanwhile we wait for its restoration,
invoking it with all our skill—
because without it
all the organizing fails,
and I will not
quite
catch your not
quite
catching me.

Easter Island

I EMBARKATION

Some have named this space where we are rooted
a place of death.
We fix them with our callous eyes
and call it, rather, a terrain of resurrection.
Love, we maintain, is more complex than theory,
is incorrect, absurd, miraculous, a contradiction,
senseless, intricate, murderous—a mystery.

Clever, but too easy, to hypothesize love
as that process by which the beloved's arbitrary face
is kindly interposed between the lover and her fear
of inattentive chaos, a universe monotone, arrythmic,
bald as the open sea.

What if, I say, a beloved face gave no such quarter
but so transluded itself into a conductor for that very sight:
eyes mandalan, primeval,
forehead opening and closing like a sea anemone
undulant for the prey startled by such loveliness,
nostrils sucking at some ether
alien from this air the lover gasps,
mouth yawing syllabic reminiscences of a lost home,
vast, empty, meaningless.

This is not pretty.
This is not *useful*, one might argue,
leaving aside outgrown romantic hypocrisies
and focusing on struggle.
We are mature now.

                                        / / /

I am not a fool, even a holy fool.
I have wanted to settle for nothing.
I have wanted to become mature as the dolphin is mature:
a pacific complex intelligence communicating mutual mysteries
while wearing an inexhaustible wry smile;
a fish that breathes oxygen and can fly,
an underwater mammal, a dumb beast with language—
a contradiction; a witty shape at home
both in air vault and sea plunge;
monogamous with her mate for life, one with her community.
Look how she streaks her glossy understatement
like a sign, a covenant between sky and water,
an exuberant arc celebrating nothing but itself
against the gravity of blue hemming in flatter blue.

This is miraculous, but not useful.
I am not a fool nor, sadly, a mature dolphin.
I am just a woman, thirty-three years old,
trying to be useful, focusing on struggle.
Here is a man. Notice his forehead, his eyes.
He is not a fool, either.

Then there are explorers, those who would try to map us,
who want only my detailed condemnation
of this man, this struggle,
the correct impossibility of this love.
They are relieved at each clue that leads, they think,
to understanding their own pain.
It is perilous to find one's way in a city
with the guidebook to an island of volcanic rock.
We are all more intricate than that, more lost.
I must not exhort them with simplicities again,

or permit them this: that what I risk exposing
—dead ends, short cuts, failure, exhaustive new excursions—
that these be calcified to proof
so they can claim, self-satisfied, that as they thought
the whole time, it could not be done.

This man, remember, is also not a fool,
and not, regrettably, a dolphin.
Each time they label, simplify, degrade, or chart my paleoglyphs,
impulsive, he erupts against such dogma;
their undertow of simple-mindedness
becomes a murderous riptide in his wake.
Wait. This is absurd.
If I call him murderer, it is them I fear,
their conclusions, correct lies of support that would drown him
before I could describe what else lies inland
from the shore's treachery.

What else. Year on year of sustenance, challenge, love?
Abstractions for that which resonates between us like a covenant,
unapproachable by trails of overnight analysis.
Concretions, more: molten stone thrombotic from the earth,
breathed into bedrock by our will.
This, at least: what is at stake here
is not superficial.
Support was to have been
more intricate than jargon.

Here is a man who longs for a love poem
less than my breath, inextricable from his,
its oxygen a blessing borne by trade winds.
This is deserved. That is incorrect.

/ / /

Here are some others, you perhaps, most men, even some women
(not all, to be sure), who thirst for the bracing poems of hate,
uncomplicated at last as the sheer refreshing force of tropic rain.
This is deserved. That is senseless.
These are contradictions.

Because he is murderous.
Because they are murderous.
Because I murder these truths, speaking in cinders,
ash approximating what is fireflow.

I am a woman, thirty-three years old, who would be useful.
But love is more complex than theory.
The flattening rains ride on the trade winds,
they come at once, they alternate:
I suck at the wind and my face is wet.
How can I constrict this message
so it will be understood
uneasily?

II ARRIVAL

Mariners, leaving the Netherlands where they were born,
sailed, womanless, for years
to chart the new world's waters,
sighted this island, named it a place of resurrection.
We fix them with our callous eyes
and call it, rather, a terrain of death.
We are not fools.

/ / /

There are theories, none proven,
about these paleoglyphs, still undeciphered,
about these monolithic statues—
each an immensity, a brooding human face
carved from tufa, scoria, volcanic rock;
each weighing almost eight tons,
each looming near forty feet.

Some say these are the ruined deities
of a civilization more ancient than the Aztec.
Some say they are quite recent, merely
six or seven hundred years' duration,
sculpted by the Polynesians as island sentinels.
Some even say they wait, stoic as artifacts,
for the return of visitors from a distant planetary family
who carved the creatures in their image.
None can explain what leverage
could have placed such massive stones in these positions.

But love is senseless, murderous, a mystery.
All we suspect is that once, an impulsive hemorrhage of lava
for no useful reason, here, in the middle of the ocean,
bled liquid rock, layer on tier on stratum on water on air on sand
into an island, brought forth papaya and sugarcane
and tall grass in a silver tide rippling beneath trade winds,
flattened by rains, ebbing and rising above firm roots.

All we suspect is that we came to be,
crafted by some one, some culture, some unlikely distant gods,
lapicides of ourselves, perhaps, layer on year on air—
an infinitely complicated process of creation
for no reason that, so far, can be deciphered.

/ / /

But we are rooted in this space,
near one another and not touching
for the analyses of tourists and cartographers.
Our presences inhale each other's adamance.
The dignity of each is original.
Notice his mouth, my forehead.
Can a cave exhale murder?
Can a sea anemone lie?
Explorers say our lavic eyes are callous,
more remote than the accessible Mayan gaze
in all its impassivity.

We do not find this so, but then
they say we were positioned
never to see each other's face,
both imaginary stares intent, instead, on the surrounding sea.
Dolphins sometimes leap there,
unstitching the horizon's seam.
Observers have no way of knowing
if we are moved by such a sight.
It is supposed we watch, these centuries,
side by side, for nothing.
This is a contradiction.

So is the exuberance I feel
to know myself erode, grateful, gradual,
scoured by the wind and porous to the rain,
my features towering downward toward the beach
in an imperceptible release from waiting
to become again the glossed density of stone,
uncarved, expressionless.

/ / /

His unseen lithic face will also burl to pebbles
and sift with the shards of what were once myself,
inextricable sand at last,
none of us useful.

Meanwhile, for now, this must suffice:
that murder and resurrection are the levers of change,
that creation and complexity are one,
that miracle is contradiction.

And if, in my slow deliquescence, my face seems changed,
some alteration of my features
unaccountable to simple wind and rain,
may he perceive and may they grant
at least the possibility of a love
not easily understood,
the mystery that scorian lips can briefly wear
a dolphin smile.

The Two Gretels

The two Gretels were exploring the forest.
Hansel was home,
sending up flares.

Sometimes one Gretel got afraid.
She said to the other Gretel,
"I think I'm afraid."
"Of course we are," Gretel replied.

Sometimes the other Gretel whispered,
with a shiver,
"You think we should turn back?"
To which her sister Gretel answered,
"We can't. We forgot the breadcrumbs."

So, they went forward
because
they simply couldn't imagine the way back.

And eventually, they found the Gingerbread House,
and the Witch, who was really, they discovered,
the Great Good Mother Goddess,
and they all lived happily ever after.

The Moral of this story is:

Those who would have the whole loaf,
let alone the House,
had better throw away their breadcrumbs.

The Network of the Imaginary Mother

1 THE MOTHER

"There is nothing you cannot be,"
she said crossly, "if you want to be it enough."
Momma, all her unfinished poems glued amber
on pages embrittled in notebook reliquaries;
Momma, who came a virgin to the man she loved,
who lay with him through nights when the yellow star,
his Dachau constellation, glowed again in all his dreams;
Momma, who waxed with me, the bastard daughter
he had offered to acknowledge if it were a son;
Momma, who fought for my life inside her womb
as he had fought for his outside the ovens;
who threatened to disbelieve him Jew, to call him Nazi
unless he granted me his name—and when he did,
refused it, choosing her own and mine instead
from that of Merlin's old arch-enemy,
witch-queen, sorceress.

Now she stood scrying for me whole worlds
of what no one could stop me from becoming:
art, music, science, wealth, influence, fame,
each threaded hook tugging at my child's excitement
as we fed the ducks in Bronxville Pond
and watched our bread sink upon their waters,
a propitiation to the waterlilies' soot-gray petals.
She loved Blake's etchings then, and Kafka's tales,
the *Appassionata,* and Lao-tzu's mysteries.
And I was her miracle, her lever, her weapon,
the shuttle of her loom.
I didn't mind that until later, didn't suffocate
within it yet, but loved instead the very smell

of her terrycloth bathrobe, comforting myself
with its odor of her when she had to work late
at the lingerie counter and my aunt put me to bed
before Momma returned.

   And this is the fragrance, almost forgotten,
   that warms the deepest dreams of us all—
   even the large male children who grow
   to fear, or conquer, or imitate its power;
   even the large female children who find ourselves
   rocking each other, or men, or babies—
   we, the living totems of that rhythmic breast
   that rocked us, and which we have become,
   yet long for still.

Her power—when did I begin to sense its origins?
When did I embrace my disgust
at this gross world, her fat body, my own flesh?
Was it there with the first contraction,
when my outraged head thudded stubborn
against her pelvis, turning itself aside
again, again, in my refusal to leave her?
—or when, after being dragged alive
into a sick yellow dawn by double forceps,
this matter and energy of me, unreconciled,
met in the initial skirmish of a battle to the death:
convulsions jerking the puppet baby
every four hours for the first two days?
By the age of ten I felt stayed in the corset of my ribs,
basted to my spine, sausaged into my skin.
A few years after, I would write about Icarus:

"The shed husk lies upon the ground
and one is free."
Still later, I read Teilhard de Chardin
and wept with lust for deliverance into spirit,
light, soul, intellect.
This blood was not of my making.
These breasts were not of my willing.
There is nothing you cannot be if you want it enough.

She had lied more than once.

I felt her watch me with a superfluity of eyes,
reach for me with eight arms,
spidery as an Eastern goddess.
She seemed to sit at the center of my life,
secreting my future, dividing herself
into two half-bodies, one of which was meant for me.
I fought her architecture, her manipulations,
calling her three-faced, thinking her common
though organic, and certainly original.

And all these cycles later, all the scenes
and silent intervals and tears, what is left between us?
That blood was my own, those breasts were all I knew.
They hang empty now; all her pulp sags jaundiced, flaccid,
rippling from her palsied limbs.
What is intolerable here
is the voice of a three-year-old child in me
who cries that with this death the world is ending:
Age Unlimited, the wreckers, are tearing down
my first home.
Paid by the hour, they take their time.

/ / /

Where Blake and Lao-tzu once mused,
unreformed rabbis rave, now, in her brain's asylum.
Doctors incise, lawyers unravel
her frenzied weaving of lawsuits, wills, stock-market deals.
She disowns all her transformations.
She wants to make a killing before she dies.

How can she recognize my real inheritance—
that I became an heiress long ago of her indifference
to the celebration of her own body
or another woman's, or a man's
—this, her means of enduring;
the lesson passed to me, the knot
untangled still by thirty years of patience,
by three decades of courage still uncut.
Not that this is all she gave me,
although the matriheritage left her impoverished.
She shuffles at each curb, shifting her feet
while her forehead breaks out in rhinestones of sweat:
she cannot estimate how deep the step is.
Her whole body tremors with Parkinson's
lascivious dybbuk, as if her torso
were a giant heart, pumping its spasms
along attendant arteries, her puppet limbs.
She is too strong to die of this, though—
a mere degenerative disease.

She will be murdered by attack
when one day quite soon now
a small, arteriosclerotic organ
the size of her clenched fist,
unnourished by the living current beating

hopeless in blocked passageways,
unable to release
all that congested, shameless, scarlet love
for its own body:
when one day this heart—her actual heart—implodes.
Meanwhile, she is afraid to read my poems, that best of me
I offer her—afraid she will not understand them
or afraid she will.
She waits alone with still more Yahrzeit candles each Yom Kippur,
alone, and I intransigent in my own fierce survival,
knowing at last her way is not my way.

But there must be some honor even in survival.
So when she fell and lay six hours unable to reach the phone,
and then was sped to the hospital where we—yes, They and I—
fought for weeks to break her will in order to save her life,
and when she returned, a barren invalid, to her apartment's clutter,
the lure of my blood was there before me.
Helpless, I waded upstream to where I had been born
to give her birth this time—brutal as she, after all,
merciless, bullying the medication into her decrescent body,
learning at last and bitterly and utterly:
The life comes first. There is no spirit without the form.

And this is the knowledge, almost remembered,
that chills the deepest nightmares of us all—
the grown male children who fear the wheel
is turned by Kali's dancing; the grown female
children who lose ourselves, complacent,
to only one of the Three Aspects: Virgin, Mother, Crone,
and then deny the numinous presence of the other Two
in any woman, in terror of what we are becoming,
yet long for still.

/ / /

Vile. This is vile. This is the Mystery
from which my inmost flesh-revulsion springs.
This loathing, now, to kneel between these massive thighs
squatting in pain; to bear this bedpan like a chalice
for the dregs of her life's untold hagiography;
to lie such set responses of encouragement and comfort.
Here is the truth I flee from in my own body—
the cosmic wit of each cell's purulescence:
this stench of death and urine, this bulging pubes
flecked with matted hair.
Here are your gates of eternity, your pit, your trapdoor,
your fissure in the earth before which the priestess sways.
Here is the lair of tabu, the grove of ritual.
Here I was born.

I am up to my elbows in filth,
inescapably undead.
There is no cleansing from this.
There is only rage, and the instinct older than love
that thrusts my arms in deeper,
grasping the life that is her, is myself,
the spirit raining pus for iridescence,
the infection of being alive
which I shall never again disclaim.

Momma, I will be with you when you die.

> *Repeat the syllables*
> *until the lesson is drummed along the arteries:*
> *Margaret Jones, midwife, hanged 1648.*
> *Joan Peterson, veterinarian, hanged 1652.*

/ / /

Isobel Insch Taylor, herbalist, burned 1618.
Mother Lakeland, healer, burned 1645.

What have they done to you?

2   THE CONSORT

Say what you will, there is this man.
Correct or incorrect, father-figure, faggot, fool,
or any other pat conclusion you assume be damned.
There is this man.
I who hate the class of men have loved this man
for almost half my life. Nothing,
not even him, will stop me now.
Certain things are understood between us.

Yes, I was seventeen, and suicidal, and a poet.
Yes, he was ten years older, suicidal, and a poet.
(We may be suicidal but we're hardly self-destructive.)
It was the bond of poetry no one could comprehend:
that what his mind contained appeared to me
as an interior castle, its crystal terraced
radiant through the body I desired and feared.
The litanies of struggle, of despair, I've intoned elsewhere
and doubtless will again: once to have said such things
was thought unspeakable.
Unfashionable, now, to sing:
radiant, you see, spirit in matter,
pulsant with energy, the word made flesh.

                                                          / / /

Say what you will, I was not wrong.

This is now the thirteenth year
since I came virgin to him, to the one man
I have loved, since I first lay with him
through nights when all his lovers
haunted our dream-streets, mocking their maleness and his;
averting their eyes from me, his transgression,
his sin—my body the glowing sign
of his desertion from their numbers.
This is the thirteenth year
since that cheap votive candle stuttered its light
on the bedsheet where my ritual blood
pooled like wax for the signet of our embrace.

See, these are the poems we tore from one another,
these are the scars.
The stitches have been absorbed.
At first I knew only his power.
At first he set his seal upon me.
At first he could not have known my power
or understood the misuse of his own.
At first we were drawn solely by what we would become.

But this is the thirteenth year,
and we are drawn by what we have always been,
always, before breath, poems, dreams
could inhabit us.
Now is my seal set upon him,
as it was in the beginning
when we foamed up from my imagination, infinite,
and exploded into our innumerable selves.

/ / /

Here is your matter and energy,
your electrons and protons.
Here is my ecstatic whim, primordial,
the DNA pattern purled light-speed from my needles;
the immaculate violent ordure of this cauldron
from which all entities crawl—

the insouciant earthworm, the maga clam
who divides herself,
experiments with making that part
of her macro-organismic possibility
male,
the complement, the consort,
the curious delightful novelty of him.

He approaches his tryst, the arthropodiacal lover:
        Eager to please, he proudly tiptoes, eight-legged,
                toward me on the surface of the waters.
                He offers food.
                If I accept the gift, his courtship may begin.
        Eager to amuse, he jumps in his excitement,
                waving gaudy striped legs, hopping in self-congratulation
                at having found me.
        Eager to arouse, he sidles in a cunning rhythm
                near where I may observe him; he pantomimes
                how he would wrap me loosely
                in a special mating canopy of silk.
Spinning, I cast down my dragline for his ascent.
I disown none of my transformations.

And ever since,
leisurely, through all the thirteen orphic eternities,

we have been quickening toward each other
in this saraband:
    Exchanging lanquidities with our lama eyes;
    Keening a seaweed counterpoint in our great blue whale voices
        across the ocean's amphitheaters;
    He, his electric-maned head suddenly lifted, nostrils flaring
        to catch the lioness scent of me whole deserts distant;
    I centripetaling down my ladder of air, drawn by the beacon-fire
        his feathers spread for me in a strutting audition—
        such phosphorescent greens and violets;
    Salt mellow on our tongues from tasting each other's
                                  skin and tears.
Ever since, a floating through sameness and difference,
poems like sparks of laughter
struck from the flint of our diversionary griefs.
This is possible.
I have said so.

He has feared I divide myself, divide him:
mind and body, spirit and flesh, the cosmic and the daily.
As if I could settle for nothing.
I say to him, yes, there are certain reasons
I have chosen this—among them, choicelessness;
as if the center of my life were knotted up
into a hub of memory, itself unspeakable,
from which is spoken all that moves me.
I say to him that such a clot will never be dissolved
except along paths radiating order
which only then can be ignored—as each spoke
must be balanced with precision on a wheel
in preparation merely to blur invisible
once the wheel spins.

                      / / /

The means and goal must justify each other.
For how many millennia must the river sculpt the canyon?
How opaque must the winter sleep become
before Northern Lights visit the eye?
I say to him:
Why have I called you "Mother" in my dreams?

> And this is the question, almost unwhispered,
> that wakens the riddled nights of us all—
> the grown male children who dare not yet answer
> what the grown female children yet dare not ask:
> where is the reason for loving? who risked inventing it?
> how large must we grow before giving birth to each other,
> a labor we fear to begin each dawn,
> yet long for still.

I affirm all of my transformations.

For this is the thirteenth year
and I am come into my power.

I say to him:
There is a place beyond our struggle
where I will take us—
beyond the archetypal, the animal,
even the human,
beyond all we have been so far.
It will exist, see, I am creating it now.
You are utterly given over unto me.
And I will make of you the beloved,
I will call sacred antlers up from your brow
and place pipes against your lips.

/ / /

Your haunches are mine, your sly buttocks,
your body disarrayed of all but my arms' garlands,
your brain encelled with my brain, double lotus.
Before your Osirian trance will I unveil myself.
You shall be again the luminous bridegroom
all my suffering foresaw—
upon whose groin I placed my palm
to consecrate the light that streamed
from all your prophecies.

We shall never be finished.
I name you
husbandman.
I say:
There is this man.
I claim him.
Blessed be, it is he I have chosen.

      Repeat the syllables
      until the lesson is pumped through the heart:
      Nicriven, accused of lasciviousness, burned 1569.
      Barbara Gobel, described by her jailors
          as "the fairest maid in Wurzburg,"
          burned 1629, age nineteen.
      Frau Peller, raped by Inquisition torturers
          because her sister refused
          the witch-judge Franz Buirman, 1631.
      Maria Walburga Rung, tried at a secular court
          in Mannheim as a witch,
          released as "merely a prostitute,"
          accused again by the episcopal court

at Eichstadt, tortured into confession,
and then burned alive, 1723, age twenty-two.

What have they done to me?

3 THE SISTER

There are these women's faces, a montage
of features so like my own, though darker or older
or thinner or sweeter. They have names each,
and unique identical secrets. Lady of the Sorrows.
Lady of the Plants. Lady of the Scales.
These are my people.
The lattice of my spine shudders with such a weight.

There are these women's faces, various
as dewprints sequined across my life's web,
every grain reflecting a different dawn.
The interlace of all my years shudders with such a weight
until each pod of moisture bursts,
flooding toward the center—
that hub of memory, itself unspeakable,
from which is spoken all that moves us.

There is this woman's face,
she for whom I have spun out of myself
whole networks of survival.
"Each with the one weapon the other most needed
at that moment."
Who could have dreamt that the weapons
simply would be ourselves,

placed each in the other's keeping?
The love that, once, did not dare speak its name
may lie in silence yet for reasons other
than even you and I assume—life and death reasons
beyond a mere surviving.

Perhaps if these six years that lie behind us
had not also lain between us,
perhaps if we had not met one spring equinox too late,
perhaps I might have sung then
what since I have been forced to whisper
in too many bad translations, a luxury
of plain details, such as:
—My dear, that birthmark high on your right cheek
actually is a virus, the devil's stamp
they would have called it once, a life form improbable
as an albino olive blithely afloat
in a cup of its own goldgreen Nile oil.
Your eyelids are Mycenean; they cradle
the fertile crescents of your eyes—
perhaps.

Instead, the ancient tragedy of women closed around us,
our version identical with every other, unique
only in minute details of Eleusinian translation
reenacted, even as my arms reached to close round you
—the daughter I thought I'd found,
the mother I thought I'd lost,
O Demeter, O Kore—
then something rose and walked again in me
and would not let me rest until
I could stand scrying for you worlds
of what no one could stop you from becoming,

until you were my miracle, my lever, the shuttle
of my loom, you not even minding that,
not suffocating in it, yet.

When did you begin to sense my power?
Your own was so different, so indifferent,
alive with reckless sensuality
to answer all my sentience.
You would freeze me on camping trips,
contort me into yoga knots,
melt me in hot-springs baths,
hammering like a metronome against my fugue
your signature: the physical.
And all the while my wondering
if you were part of this plot that would embody me.

If so, then move by move, and all but motionless,
I still have beaten you at chess, by god.
I have wrenched your brain into places
you fancied I might.
I have mourned with you
and I have densified myself into a magnet
strong as you always demanded it to be,
stronger than you intended to resist.
When the holy sea-mammal gives birth
there is another dolphin, the dolphin-midwife
they call her, to attend and to assist the labor.
So I tracked you, relentless,
to where you patiently fled my arrival.

Our peril was more complicated
even than you and I assumed,

though cowards will see in our love
their own lovelessness, yet remain ignorant
of what we know: to be afraid can be a moral act.

We thought ourselves such careful weavers.
We never meant to choose our pattern
from the marble of that Aegean figure:
the goddess daughter statued on the goddess mother's head—
yet history let no other model stand for us
unbroken or reclaimed: even those two women
exchanging gifts on the Pharsalian stele,
a balance of sisters who appear equals of each other
and of the task as well—these two are also
Demeter and Kore.

And so I saw myself begin to watch you
with a superfluity of eyes,
felt you reach for me as with eight arms,
until I came to sit at the center of your life,
secreting your future, dividing myself
into two half-bodies, one of which was meant for you.
At times you fought my architecture, my manipulations.
At other times you cried without me that the world was ending.
There is nothing you cannot be if you want it enough, I said.

And this is the prophecy, almost ignored,
that lies like a truth beneath our desiring to will
our will to desire: the large male children
who would secretly conquer themselves in each other;
the grown female children who would rather not conquer
at all, even those selves we flee in disgust from,
yet long for still.

                         / / /

Now must your seal be set upon yourself.
Another "must"? Another.
To nurture what we have delivered,
you must spin networks of survival
all of your own imagining.
Then, then it can be said
that you are beautiful to me
as the rare flower of a roseate cactus,
your loveliness wild as a blizzard of mountain snow,
your smile lazy and then sudden as the dance of a young lizard.

Now, like a sybil, I can see
that where you walk, a new Persephone blinking in the light,
tendrils verdant with possibilities
tremble awake, there, in your footprints.
One bears an orb of tiny flowers,
a circlet of lace pale as the new moon's pledge,
a sable star at its heart,
sealing the cancellation of all debts between us—

that this release might teach us both
how all my mother posturing and all your daughter mime
was played out after all by siblings, the grown female children
of an older One whose quick sagacity
has watched us with more than a single pair of eyes:
air-breathing arachnid, She whose body
is divided into two equal, balanced parts,
whose hidden spinnerets secrete a liquid
the air hardens into silk
as useful for wrapping eggs as luring enemies,
for knitting gossamer balloons from which to swing while riding
summer's currents to her chosen destination—

and oh, for wreathing the symmetry of a mandala,
this other network, original, organic
as a common orb-web, its quatro-corners
anchored to fire, water, earth, and air,
radiant from the hub whose spokes unspeakably
still move us.

No longer Demeter in such a different dawn, Persephone,
I feel my gaze endewed with prisms
through which I watch that hub, those spokes,
shiver, then slowly pivot, then spin free,
blurring into its revolution
The World Disc, The Great Round,
The Silver Wheel of Transformation,
within which your own life must hurtle—
one brief arc deathless as a single head
of Queen Anne's lace,
plucked from my root self involuntary as a poppy,
and lightly twirled between the palms—
a token of welcome and farewell,
a seal,
a small gift
from one woman
to another.

>   *Repeat the syllables*
>   *before the lesson hemorrhages through the brain:*
>   *Margaret Barclay, crushed to death with stones, 1618.*
>   *Mary Midgely, beaten to death, 1646.*
>   *Peronette, seated on a hot iron as torture*
>   *and then burned alive, 1462.*
>   *Sister Maria Renata Sanger, sub-prioress*

of the Premonstratensian Convent of Unter-Zell,
accused of being a lesbian;
the document certifying her torture
is inscribed with the seal of the Jesuits,
and the words Ad Majorem Dei Gloriam—
To the Greater Glory of God.

What have they done to us?

4   THE CHILD

Hush.
This is utterly simple.
Before you,
I did not know what it meant to love.
I did not know it was this:

> Your outraged head
> thudding stubborn against my pelvis,
> turning itself aside again, again,
> in your refusal to leave me.

> The absolutism of your eyelids,
> lilac-veined transparencies that swell
> in rhythm to the rolling of your dream.

> The authority of your mouth;
> its gravity, tongue-frail,
> drawing up the tide from my lunar nipples.

/ / /

The visitation of that laugh
you abandon me to, unasked for, sudden,
miraculous as an underground spring
unlocking the Februaries of my life.

The summer-nap smell of your body,
the grace with which you stretch on wakening, animal,
the vulnerability of your baby penis, a rosehip
blooming shameless under my all unthreatened kiss.

This blood is my own, of my own making.
Flesh of my flesh. These breasts were all you knew.
Before this, I did not understand
the luxury of skin, its velvet imperative.
You have taught me
the most ancient of pleasures.

In awe of this
have we been celebrated from the first:
the Hittite lion-mother, brazen above her child;
the Isis, hammered in copper, cupping her left breast
toward where you lean up from her lap;
the pre-Columbian effigy vessels where I smile
at your marsupial grasp;
the Yoruban wood-spools; the Celtic icons, stone-hewn;
the prehistoric bronze Sardinian pietà;
the scaraboid seal, Ionian, on which I whelp you;
the Aztec codex of the goddess Tlazolteotl;
the fifteenth-century "Vierge Ouvrante"—that virgin
whose enthroned self opens as two doors, disclosing
the world, safe, sleeping, on her knees.

/ / /

And this is the reason, always denied,
that throbs like an uncut cord through the warp
of our fantasies: the large male children
who adopt each other in defiance;
the grown female children who reject the mothers
we once were—before they became the only selves
we were permitted to become,
yet long for still.

I disown
none
of my transformations.

Little heart, little heart,
you have sung in me like the spiral alder-bud.
You, who gave birth to this mother
comprehend—for how much longer?—my mysteries.
Son of my cellular reincarnation, you alone know
the words that awaken me when I play dead
in our game. You alone wave
at the wisp through which I see you.
You understand. You whisper,
"Listen—life is really going on, right now,
around us. Do you see it? Sometimes I lose it
but if I sit still and listen, it comes back,
and then I think, How funny, this is what being alive is.
Do you know?"
I have uttered you wisely.

Still, I have grieved before the time, in preparation
for my dolor, at how you will become
a grown male child, tempted by false gods.

                                    / / /

I have been *Pisaura mirabilis,* the nursery-web spider
who carries her egg's bulk in aching jaws,
who warps it in a weft of love,
who guards its hatching.
You have clung to me like a spiderling
to the back of the *Lycosa lenta;* Wolf-spider mother,
I have waited, whenever you fell off,
for you to scramble on again before proceeding.

But you have come five-fold years
and what I know now is nothing
can abduct you fully from the land where you were born.
I am come into my power, oh littlest love,
fruit of my flowering. I have seen you,
who feared the spinner less than her hoop's fragility
—fabric of nightmares—hold your breath at the rush of beauty
on a country dawn when we beheld her dew-glazed gauze corona.
You reached past fear, through reverence, to touch—
anointing your fingertips,
anointing all my August droughts.
And I have seen you, crowned by ivy leaves,
dance naked in a candlelit circle of stones,
your laughter offered to me like a bell cluster,
like the fat purple grapes you pelt me with,
your milk-teeth seducing my ear with nibbles.

Wars have been made against me, empires built
with the dolmen of my bones, ships have pocked
the egg of my covenant where it gleams
on their benighted path.
But there is no erasing this:
the central memory of what we are

to one another, the grove of ritual.
I have set my seal upon you.

I say:
you shall be a child of the mother
as of old, and your face will not be turned from me.
Then shall the bosom of the earth open and feed you,
rock you, safe, sleeping, on her lap.
No more will your stomachs bulge tumorous with hunger,
my children; no more will you be gaily tossed
on the soldiers' bayonet-points; no more will you scream
at the iron roar of death in the heavens;
no more will you stare through the miniature convulsions
of your newborn heroin addiction.
You shall be disinherited of all these legacies.
And in their place,
and in your footprints,
tendrils green with possibility will tremble
awake.

This you have taught me—what it is to love.
Your unmodern wisdom thudding against my pelvis,
refusing to leave me.
How can I not celebrate
this body,
your first home?

I did not know
how simple this secret would be.
How utterly simple.
Hush.

/ / /

Repeat the syllables
before the lesson perforates the uterus:
Anna Rausch, burned 1628, twelve years old.
Sybille Lutz, burned 1628, eleven years old.
Emerzianne Pichler, tortured and burned together
    with her two young children, 1679.
Agnes Wobster, drowned while her small son was forced
    to watch her trial by water, 1567.
Annabelle Stuart, burned alive, 1678,
    fourteen years old.
Veronica Zerritsch, compelled to dance
    in the warm ashes of her executed mother,
    then burned alive herself, 1754,
    thirteen years old.
Frau Dumler, boiled to death in hot oil
    while pregnant, 1630.

What have they done?

5   THE SELF

Each unblinking eyelet linked now
to another in the shuttles of the loom.
"Thin rainbow-colored nets, like cobwebs,
all over my skin."
I affirm
all
of my transformations:

        An autumnal mother, treading the way of life
            past all her trials, yearns toward her Albion,
            leperous-white as waterlilies.

                                    / / /

Returning to herself, a daughter who reflects
a different dawn emerges, reckless as the weeds
that array her vernal equinox.
The chosen man, given over at last, discards his
shroud
for love's reweaving, initiate to what
the ecstatic Widow male has always known, the
secret
of the young king at winter solstice—
And so is birthed again, shameless, laughing,
to reach past fear through reverence, to touch
what it is like, this being alive.
These are my people.

They are of my willing, of my own making.
I have invented them no less than I create myself,
thought imagining shape, uttering existence.
To understand this universe I fabricate
—my cosmic joke, embodied plot—
I am become the Spinner, giving out of myself
myself the Egg,
taking into myself
myself the Prey.

Witch-queen, sorceress,
I must live within this body, my final home—
here to decode each runic fingerprint,
to trust the assurance of each hair's whitening,
to recognize the clue left by each stretch-mark.
My taste is salty, my smell ammonial.
My knuckles can crack like willow-bark

and hairblades cover my hide
stubborn as fine grass.
My nails are crisp as relics
and every crevice—armpits, crotch,
toe-valleys, ears, mouth, nostrils, eyes—exudes
mucus or sweat for iridescence.
Oh let me learn that I am beautiful to me,
innocent as the spider—
beyond judgment, disgust, beyond perfection—
reconciled with her tufted claw,
with the matted topaz of my labia.
Let me sit at the center of myself
and see with all my mouths,
feel with all my setae,
know my own sharp pleasure,
learning at last and blessedly and utterly:
The life comes first. There is no spirit without the form.

Drawn from the first by what I would become,
I did not know how simple this secret could be.
The carapace is split,
the shed skin lies upon the ground.
I must devour the exoskeleton of my old shapes,
wasting no part, free only then
to radiate whatever I conceive,
to exclaim the strongest natural fiber known
into such art, such architecture
as can house a world made sacred by my building.
Sheet method, funnel, and orb,
each thread of the well-named Ariadna
unreels its lesson:

The Triangle web, three-faced as my aspects;
the filmy dome web, a model firmament;
the domesticity of the Bowl-and-Doily web;
the droll zig-zag of the Filistata;
the Hammock pattern's indolence;
the Coras web, with healing power for welts and fever;
the Trapdoor web, shield of the White Lady from the desert;
the Arabesca, the Dictyna;
the vaporous Platform web;
the Umbrella's unfolding tension;
the esoteric Pyramid design;
the Purse web, tubed and tightly wattled;
the Bubble web, patience iterated underwater,
a crystal castle of air.

Here is discipline, imagination, variation.
Here are your paragons, my avatars.

I am learning.
The cord is wrapped around my throat.
I am learning.
The passageway is cramped and blind
I am learning
though Kali dances through it, past
where Demeter still seeks Persephone,
where Isis searches for the fragments of Osiris,
where I wade upstream through a living current
that seizes me and drowns me into life,
pumping, pumping, as from a giant heart
whose roar I have called Mother in my dreams.

> *What do you remember?*
> *What is it that you long for still?*

/ / /

Oh let me hear you hear
me speak oh
speak to
me oh let me

> *Repeat the syllables*
> *each cell has unforgotten:*
> *There was the Word before their word.*
> *The Silence came.*
> *The Name was changed.*

> *What have they done to themselves?*

What have they dared,
sucking at man's wounds for wine,
celebrating his flesh as food?
Whose thirst has been slaked by his vampire liquor,
whose hunger answered by his ghostly bread?

> *Who have they dared to hang on that spine instead*
> *and then deny, across millennia?*
> *Whose is the only body which incarnates creation*
> *everlasting?*

As it was in the beginning,
    I say:
    Here is your sacrament—

> Take. Eat. This is my body,
> this real milk, thin, sweet, bluish,
> which I give for the life of the world.
> Like sap to spring it rises

even before the first faint cry is heard,
an honest nourishment
alone able to sustain you.

I say:
Here is your eternal testament—

This cup, this chalice, this primordial cauldron
of real menstrual blood
the color of clay warm with promise,
rhythmic, cyclical, fit for lining the uterus
and shed for many,
for the remission of living.

Here is your bread of life.
Here is the blood by which you live in me.

The World Disc, The Great Round,
The Wheel of Transformation.
Two solstices, summer and winter.
Two equinoxes, spring and fall.
One day to stand outside the year, unutterable.
Thirteen-fold is my lunar calendar,
Five-fold my mysteries, my kiss,
Three-fold my face.

And this is the secret, once unquestioned,
sought in the oldest trances of us all:
the large male children forced into exile
from their pelvic cradle, wailing, refusing to leave;
the grown female children, knotting together the skein
of generations, each loop in the coil a way back

to that heart of memory we cannot escape,
yet long for still.

No more need you dream this, my children,
in remembrance of me.
There is a place beyond your struggle
where I will take us.
It will exist, see, I am creating it now.
I have said so.

      Blessed be my brain
          that I may conceive of my own power.
      Blessed be my breast
          that I may give sustenance to those I love.
      Blessed be my womb
          that I may create what I choose to create.
      Blessed be my knees
          that I may bend so as not to break.
      Blessed be my feet
          that I may walk in the path of my highest will.

Now is the seal of my vision
set upon my flesh.

You call me by a thousand names, uttering yourselves.

      Earthquake I answer you, flood and volcano flow—
          the Warning.
      This to remind you that I am the Old One
      who holds the Key, the Crone to whom all things return.

                / / /

Lotus I answer you, lily, corn-poppy, centripetal rose—
        the Choice.
        This to remind you that I am the Mother
        who unravels from herself the net sustaining you.

Moon I answer you, my gibbous eye, the regenerating carapace,
        the Milky Way—
        the Possibility.
        This to remind you that I am the Virgin
        born only now, new, capable of all invention.

I have been with you from the beginning,
utterly simple.
I will be with you when you die,
say what you will.
We shall never be finished.
This is possible,
a small gift, hush.

There is nothing I have not been,
and I am come into my power.

There is nothing I cannot be.

La Dona Sebastiana

This face and body, carved from a tree,
resemble the real me.

Wood skeleton, not bone.
Wood skull, not calcium.
Sap-seep, not marrow or gluey blood.
See the grain in her forehead,
the understated knotholes of her temples.

La Dona Sebastiana,
Lady of Arrows,
what village genius whittled your death-size perfection,
moderating your radical nakedness
with only a cloak of unbleached linen,
your bald extremism with hair of plaited straw?
You smile no answer.

They build you every year
for Holy Week, for the Procession
of Penitentés
in the older villages of Mexico and Peru.
They carve you a small oak cart as well,
in which you are reverently drawn
through the streets, silent with people,
through the world.

They heap the cart with flowers
extravagant as skin.
But the economical angle of your arm
bears only wheat sheaves.
You are not fooled.

/ / /

None may reach out to touch you
but the legend tells
that each Procession your sheaf will brush one
—only one—
in the waiting crowd.
And that one will never fear again,
so blessed by the grazing of the Lady of Death.
What more is there to fear?

Two days later, they burn
the cart, the wheat, the dried flowers,
the planed geometry of you,
to celebrate the resurrection of their christ.
They have done this for three thousand years,
have built you, borne you, burned you
when Bethlehem was not yet settled.
They no longer know why.

But I know why, La Dona Sebastiana,
Woman of Wood and Wheat,
Lady of Death.

I first heard your cartwheels'
cobbled rhythm
when I was five years old,
waiting in bed one night.

As a young girl,
I glimpsed your silhouette flash near
in glances between sleep and waking.
I have felt alien here
a long time.

/ / /

And lately, I have breathed their rotting flowers
as penance,
have felt my hair-ends split like straw.

Dona Sebastiana,
Mother of Trees and Grain,
Mother of Death,
I have been an orphan now for enough seasons
where you left me, a foundling
on this doorstep.
I want my heritage.

I want my head plucking silence
like a pic on the strings of your ribs.
I want my fingers rising from the dirt
as wheat.
I am alien, alien here.

But I am patient, disciplined
as a village artisan.
I know better than to reach for you,
a vulgar grasp at what will come to me.
I am your daughter.

For you have brushed me, Lady,
claimed me for your own
as lightly as a spear of wheat
ruptures the air,
as irreversible.

There is still the end of the Procession,
and the dismantling, and the fire.

/ / /

But I, your solitary child, at least am where
I know now
they can never save me.

F R O M

Death Benefits

1 9 8 1

Death Benefits

What might I do to get beyond
living all these lives of quiet
courage too close for comfort
to endurance or mere suffering
or graceless martyrdom—all of which
equal cowardice: the unsaid, undone, unheard,
unthought of, and undreamt undoing of what
I've undeniably understood
this undertaking would unfold
or even (unconventionally) unify?

"Leave your loved ones
fixed for life," the saying goes—and stays.
Life insurance and death benefits
are what a sensible person hopes for.

Meanwhile, Denial
leaks from our containment vessels
and passes through the doors and walls
of houses, flats, lungs, conversations,
an odorless, tasteless, non-discriminating
equal opportunity destroyer,
the blinded head proud in its even,
ceaseless, swivel.

Is it Denial then I follow in a burst
of irritation with my own obsessive focus
on one subject: this man, this woman, their
tiresome and pretentiously embattled love?
Others are aging and dying, sharing a crisis
of energy, sickening, telling kind lies,
outgrowing commitments, not getting involved.

/ / /

Others, long starved into hatred, are killing
still others with the death benefit that reassures
them they are not merely part of a tactical phase.
Others glide through back alleys, blunted
triangles of shadow, movable famines, bolts
of coarse cloth whispering How disrespectful
to god it would be to appear
out in public not wearing scar tissue.
Besides, it's protective, they add, turning
away. Why is that swivel familiar?

How can Denial deny coexisting
with the fiddlehead fern even as it exudes
its own Bach Air for cello too loud
for our ears? Or, wordless, deny
how a cat celebrates its own tongue
with each suave coral yawn? Still,
before Affirmation becomes a denial
remember that this time cat, frond, and
melody too will be forced
to share benefits deadly as our own
denial of what they have never protested to be
their own innocence: too pure for that.

Which is not a disclaimer. I too have had policies,
kept up my payments, gone veiled, benefited
from death—and denial of death.
And thought of cashing it in, more than once,
really fixing my loved ones for life,
escaping now, here, eluding what's due to me
anyway on its maturity, swiveling once and for all

beyond any benefits I could accrue
through denial of what is denied to be life.

To deny that insurance, of course, breaks
the scar tissue open, leaking what we yet could
say, do, hear, think of, understand, dream
from the containment, leaking a different
radiance over bared heads.

What might I do then to get beyond
dying so many lives of affirming Denial?
Who is this figure I swivel behind like a shadow?
Who are the woman and man I'm being drawn back to—
again, the flaw here, the fall now, the original
schism, the atom entire?

Policies lapse. Nothing is sure
any longer. That fact alone is
a renegade benefit, something like grace,
green, mimetic, audacious—daring to bleed,
sing, embrace simply each other, to find
in those arms a planet entire, swiveling up
its azure, full face,
blinking new eyes, yawning into a loud
rain of relief to be home. Almost as if,
this late, unveiled and forgiven, even
Denial might weep again. And if not here,
where, you ask; if not now, when? Oh my dear,
who am I to deny?

Battery

The fist meets the face as the stone meets water.
I want to understand the stone's parabola
and where the ripples disappear,
to make the connections, to trace
the withholding of love as the ultimate violence.

Battery: a word with seven letters, seven definitions:

1) Any unit, apparatus, or grouping
in which a series or set of parts or components
is assembled to serve a common end.
2) *Electrical.* One or more primary or secondary cells
operating together as a single source of direct current.
3) *Military.* A tactical artillery unit.
4) *A game position.* In baseball, the pitcher
and catcher together.
5) *Law.* The illegal beating or touching of another person.
6) *Music.* The percussion instruments of an orchestra.
7) *Optics.* The group of prisms in a spectroscope.

I want to understand the connections
—between the tower where Bertha Mason Rochester
is displayed to Jane Eyre as a warning
—with this place, this city, my doorstep
where I've learned to interfere between
the prostitute's scream and the pimp's knife
is to invite their unified disgust.

I want to understand the components:
—the stone's parabola, the percussion instruments,
the growth of battered children into battered wives
who beat their children,

—the beating of the fallow deer in Central Park Zoo
by unknown teenage assailants,
—the beating of these words against the poem:
to hit, slap, strike, punch, slash, stamp,
pound, maul, pummel, hammer, bludgeon, batter—
to hurt, to wound,
to flex the fist and clench the jaw and withhold love.

I want to discover the source of direct current,
to comprehend the way the primary or secondary cells
operate together as that source:
—the suburban community's defense of the fugitive Nazi
discovered to be a neighbor,
—the effect of her father's way with women
on the foreign policy of Elizabeth Tudor,
—the volunteers for a Utah firing squad;
the manner in which kwashiorkor—Red Johnny,
the Ghanaians call this slow death by starvation—
turns the hair of children a coppery color
with the texture of frayed wire.

I want to follow the refractions of the prism:
—the water's surface shuddering in anticipation
of the arching pebble,
—the oilslick mask imposed on the Pacific,
—the women of the Irish peace movement accused
of being traitors to tactical artillery units on both sides,
and replying, "We must accept that
in the next few months we will become their targets."
—The battering of dolphins against tuna nets,
—the way seloscia, a flower commonly known

as coxcomb, is bulbous, unpetaled, and a dark velvet red—
and always reminds me of a hemorrhaging brain.

The danger in making the connections
is to lose the focus,
and this is not a poem about official torture
in Iran or Chile or the Gulag, or a poem about
a bald eagle flailing its wings as it dies,
shot down over Long Island.
This is a poem called "Battery" about a specific woman
who is twelve-going-on-seventy-three and who
exists in any unit, grouping, class, to serve a common end.
A woman who is black and white and bruised all over
the world, and has no other place to go
—while the Rolling Stones demand shelter
—and some cops say it's her own fault for living with him
—and some feminists say it's her own fault for living with him;
and she hides her dark red velvet wounds
from pride, the pride of the victim,
the pride of the victim at not
being the perpetrator,
the pride of the victim at not knowing how
to withhold love.

The danger of fixing on the focus
is to lose the connections, and this is a poem
about the pitcher and the catcher *together:*
—the battery of Alice Toklas, conversing cookbooks
with the other wives while Gertrude Stein shared her cigars
and her ideas with the men,
—the sullen efficiency of Grace Poole,
—the percussion of my palm striking my husband's face

in fury when he won't learn how to fight back, how to outgrow
having been a battered child, his mother's battered wince
rippling from his eyes, his father's laborer's fingers
flexing my fist, the pitcher and the catcher together
teaching me how to withhold love;
the contempt of the perpetrator for the pride of the victim.
The collaboration, the responsibility, the intimate
violence, the fantasy, the psychic battery, the lies,
the beating of the heart.

To fear, to dread, to cower, cringe, flinch,
shudder, to skulk, to shuffle.

Wing-beat, heart-beat,
the fist meets the face as the stone displaces water,
as the elbow is dislocated from the socket
and the connections shatter from the focus;
—the knifeblade glimmers in the streetlight;
—it could be a drifting eagle feather
or cigar smoke rising
graceful as a doe who leaps in pain,
rising livid as a welt, livid as a consciousness
of my own hand falling to dispense
the bar of soap, the executioner's axe, the tuna nets,
the rifles, and at last the flint
for Bertha Mason Rochester to strike,
to spark the single source of direct current,
to orchestrate the common end emprismed
in the violent ripples of withheld love.

Batter my heart, seven-petaled word, for you
as yet but flower inside my brain;

that I may understand the stone's parabola,
make the connections, remember the focus,
comprehend the definitions,
and withhold nothing.

Peony

What appears to be
this frozen explosion of petals
abristle with extremist beauty
like an entire bouquet on a single stem
or a full chorus creamy-robed rippling
to its feet for the *sanctus*—
is after all a flower,
perishable, with a peculiar
history. Each peony
blossoms only after
the waxy casing thick around
its tight green bud is eaten literally
away by certain small herbivorous ants
who swarm round the stubborn rind
and nibble gently for weeks to release
the implosion called a flower. If
the tiny coral-colored ants have been
destroyed, the bloom cannot unfist itself
no matter how carefully forced to umbrage
by the finest hothouse gardeners.

Unrecognized, how recognizable:

Each of us nibbling discreetly
to release the flower,
usually not even knowing
the purpose, only the hunger;

each mostly unaware of any others,
sometimes surprised by a neighbor,
sometimes (so rarely) astonished

by a glimpse into one corner
at how many of us there are;

enough to cling at least, swarm back,
remain, whenever we're shaken
off or drenched away
by the well-meaning gardener, ignorant
as we are of our mission, of our being
equal in and to the task.

Unequal to the task: a word
like "revolution," to describe
what our drudge-cheerful midwifery
will bring to bear—with us not here
to see it, satiated, long since
rinsed away, the job complete.

Why then do I feel this tremble,
more like a contraction's aftermath
release, relax, relief
than like an earthquake; more
like a rustling in the belly,
or the resonance a song might make
en route from brain to larynx,
        as if now, here, unleaving itself of all
        old and unnecessary outer layers

                butterfly from chrysalis
                snake from cast skin
                crustacean from shell
                baby from placenta

something alive before
only in Anywoman's dreamings
begins to stretch, arch, unfold
each vein on each transparency opening proud,
unique, unduplicate,
each petal stiff with tenderness,
each gauzy wing a different shading flecked
ivory silver tangerine moon cinnamon amber flame
hosannas of lucidity and love in a wild riot,
a confusion of boisterous order
all fragrance, laughter, tousled celebration—
     only a fading streak like blood
     at the center, to remind us we were there once

          but are still here, who dare,
          tenacious, to nibble toward such blossoming
          of this green stubborn bud
          some call a world.

F R O M

Depth Perception

1 9 8 2

Piecing

(for Lois Sasson)

"Sometimes you don't have no control over the way
things are. Hail ruins the crops, or fire burns
you out. And then you're just given so much to
work with in a life and you have to do the best you
can with what you got. That's what piecing is.
The materials is passed on to you, or is all you
can afford. But the way you put them together is
your business. You can put them in any order you
like. Piecing is orderly."

—An anonymous woman quoted in
The Quilters: Women and Domestic Art

Frugality is not the point. Nor waste.
It's just that very little is discarded
in any honest spending of the self,
and what remains is used and used
again, worn thin by use, softened
to the pliancy and the translucence
of old linen, patched, mended, reinforced,
and saved. So I discover how
I am rejoicing slowly into a woman
who grows older daring to write
the same poem over and over, not merely
rearranged, revised, reworded, but one poem
hundreds of times anew.

The gaudy anniversaries.
The strips of colorless days gone unexamined.
This piece of watered silk almost as shot with light
as a glance he gave me once. This sturdy
canvas shred of humor. That fragment of pearl velvet,
a particular snowstorm. Assorted samples of anger—
in oilcloth, in taffeta, in tufted chenille,
in every imaginable synthetic and ready-to-wear.

/ / /

This diamond of tie-dyed flannel baby-blanket;
that other texture of deception, its dimensional embroidery.
A segment of bleached muslin still crisp with indifference.
This torn veil of chiffon, pewter as the rain
we wept through one entire July. These brightly printed
squares across which different familiar figures
walk through parks or juggle intricate abstract designs.
Two butterflies of yellow organdy my mother cut
when I was eight months old. A mango gros-grain ribbon
fading off toward peach. The corner of an old batik
showing one small window that looked out on—what?
A series of simple cotton triangles in primary colors.
And this octagonal oddment: a sunburst or mandala or pinwheel
radiating rainbow stripes against what turns out
upon close inspection to be a densely flowered background.
It's striking enough to be a centerpiece.

Once I thought this work could be less solitary.
Many of us, I imagined, would range ourselves
along the edges of some pattern we would all agree on
well beforehand, talking quietly while we worked
each with her unique stitch inward to the same shared center.

This can still be done, of course, but some designs
emerge before they can be planned, much less agreed on,
demand an entire life's work, and are best viewed upon completion.
And then, so many designers bore too easily
to work the same theme over and over, with only
the slightest gradual adjustments, like subtly changing
your thread from brown to grey.

/ / /

Still, the doorbell does toll in visitors, some of whom
slash rents across the section just perfected
—all without meaning to—
and some of whom admire the quantity or quality
of scraps, but rarely notice the order, which is
the one thing you control. But some contribute:
a quarter yard of paisley, or a length of gauze
fine enough for bandages. Once somebody left behind
an entire pocket of gold lamé, all by itself.
The challenge is to use it so
that the tarnished griefs she stuffed it with
to lend it shape need be no longer hidden.

Throwing such a piece away is not the answer. Nor
has hoarding anything to do with this.
And nobody really hazards piecework in the expectation
that someday all these fragments might inevitably
                                                    fit
into a gentle billow of warmth, to comfort
the longest winter sleep.

Not even that.
It's just the pleasure of rescuing some particle
into meaning. For a while.

Of course, this means that you yourself
are placed where you risk being
worn all the more severely
into translucent linen, held up
against the light.

Heirloom

For weeks now certain hours of every day
have been wiped sterile by the visit
to her hospital room where semi-privately
she semi-lives. For weeks
I've sourly reveled in the duty
while loathing its victim—my philanthropy
about as gracious as the bestowal of a poison cup
on a thirsty beggar who embodies a convenient excuse
but with a regrettable smell.

For days I've watched her reason fracturing
faster even than her body's fragmentation, as each
cell gradually detaches itself and shudders off
via the Parkinson method of interentropic travel.
For days the medication has made her more intense
than usual: cantankerous, weepy, domineering, sentimental,
and and and repetitive, a record that will not break
but always seems about to—the scratch on her soul itself.
No wonder she's abrasive. The wonder is,
since nothing will help her anyway,
that I can still be so ungenerous.

But then this afternoon we took each other
by surprise at the quite unexpected intersection
of Insanity and Humor—La Place de la Hallucination.
Forget that she frequently remembers I'm her sister,
or her mother, or her niece, or myself—her own child
but four years old again. Today she had some style.
Or something in me finally recognized whose style it was
I thought I'd made my own.

/ / /

The patent-leather shoe with the round white buckle
had no business being up there on the night-table, even
if it did ring so insistently. The fly that walked the track
on which the room-partitioning curtain could be pulled
was going to get run over but he refused to listen to advice.
The teensy lady who perched cross-legged on the windowsill
while wearing the whole poinsettia plant right in her hat
really should have left much earlier—but people just don't
realize how visitors can tire a popular patient out.
And whoever had sent the basket of Florida newborn babies' heads
certainly had weird taste.

And I, who should know better, who at a younger age and chemistry
than she have heard radio static stutter in strict rhyme,
flinched from a Navajo blanket that snapped its teeth at me,
watched beloved faces leer with helpful malice—
I find myself explaining to her
What Is Really There. Except she's caught me
as suddenly as I catch her, and in astonishment
I shrug and say, "You seeing 'em again, huh? Well,
whatthehell, why not. What else is there to see?"

—and miracle of bitter miracle, she laughs.
And helpless I am laughing and the semi-roommate laughs
and the invisible lady in the poinsettia hat
can be heard distinctly laughing
and in this space of semi-dying there is life
and magic and shared paranoia thicker than water
and more clear than blood and we are laughing
while the bright shoe rings
and the fly dares death
and the oranges clamor to be fed

and all the thousand spear-carrying extras
direct from Central Casting come scurrying in
got up in white to hustle us apart—
as if our waving to each other weren't a sign
beyond their understanding;
as if the giggly last whisper, "Try to get through
the night any old way you can, Love. See you
in the morning," weren't a hiccuped message
encoded too deep in each of all our lonely cells
for any deciphering.

Documentary

(Based on the documentary film *River of Sand*, by Robert Gardner, a
Phoenix Productions Film from Harvard University.)

The Hamar of Southwest Ethiopia
are the subject.

But too much stands between
for understanding, between us and this
stone-age people—an alien tribe, a dying culture,
and a geographical distance great
even in these days of Concorde.

Still, she is—how old? Not an elder,
she has no standing as an elder: she's a woman.
There is nothing that does not come between us.

"One keeps going," she says squatting,
brushing at the flies that return to her face.
"When a son is born, the father gives him a gun.
When a girl is born, the father gives her leg irons.
It's not just me." She laughs but never smiles.

"Your father wars and gives you away.
Nobody sees you. Where can you go?
You enter your husband's house a girlchild
with only your rings as your own: leg rings, rattling
arm rings. Your skirt is taken away.
In your newness you are afraid of him.
You become of his people." She says this.
I say, Everything stands surely
between us, you and I, we are not—

She describes a ceremony:
now he is old enough to beat women and girls,
to hunt, now he is a new man. Babies beat
dogs, men beat women; "cattle wear bells,
women wear bracelets, you are a rattle
in a new man's hand, you control yourself and go on."

All her front teeth have been torn out. "When
I was circumcised, you understand." She says
this, she uses the word "circumcision," not
clitoridectomy, not naming
how the sharpened shell carved out the clitoris,
the excision of pleasure, the scream
that is proof of womanhood, not speaking
the word "infibulation": the sewing up of the labia,
leaving one hole for urine and pus and menstrual fluid
to seep through, or the then forced
tearing open to ensure him virginity,
loyalty, tightness. She does not say this. I
say this, and I say, What more
could possibly stand between us, what—

> the rattle of iron bracelets, *the rattle*
> *"for decoration and for bondage"*
> she says this
> the rattle of teeth into a wooden bowl

"Women look best when scarred." She says
they say this. There are scars on her belly.
She says, "Women carry the scars earned by men
for killing an enemy. Men do not scarify themselves—
they build headdresses of clay and of ostrich plumes

and they decorate these, but men do not scar their own
flesh. It is for women to carry men's scars."
She is actually bitter, she dares to be bitter,
she laughs and snarls at her own tribe,
at the camera, she rattles like a desert snake.

"You are beaten," she says. *You are*
> *beaten as your mother was beaten.*
> *You are ground beneath the grinding stone.*
> The rattle
> of small drums, the rattle of wire whips.
> The crunch of sorghum on the grinding stone
> the rhythm.
> *"He is*

beating you even when he is not," she says.
"His whip is always in his hand, and when you run
he only sits. Where could you go?"
Everything stands everything between I am not

"You become reconciled, and that is that. Then
the husband will leave you alone." She says this aloud.
"Do women have erections or go cattle raiding
or hunting?" she laughs. "Do women have erections or kill? No,"
she rattles, "women work. Women kill lice
until the sun sets, that is how we raid. Women get wood
and go home, women haul water and work
the sorghum field. That is how we hunt.
You stay. You grind the sorghum stone,
> *you are the grinding stone,*
you touch your children and you stay."

/ / /

Too much for understanding too
great a distance—

"Men own beehives and collect honey. The leg rings
of a woman are like new beehives in a tree: they look so fine
and new." She says they say this. She says,
                    "You become of his people. Nobody sees
                    you. How can it be
                    bad? Where can you go?
Men sit on stools, drink from gourds.
Women sit on the ground. After the first birth
your husband will say, 'A child has come from between
us. Shall I then beat you forever?' "

Not her
I am not you
are not surely cannot be
we are

                    "Who does not
                    in this world practice slavery?"
                    she laughs, the toothless sophisticate.
                    "You touch the child, you stay."
Now he is old enough to beat women to show his love,
she unsmiles. *A woman may be whipped only*
by a man of the clan into which she will marry.
We are not savages, she rattles.

                    We are
not the subject, you and I. I say
this. We are not a stone-age people. We at least
try surely everything stands between

> Men jump cows, drink blood, suck marrow,
> pray for the desert flooding.

"May all be well," men say
> and spit upon the ground to make it ripe.

Women are to look best when scarred, a woman
is to be resigned into freedom only when he cannot follow
her death because she is not
> I am not
> the subject

When you die they will butter your corpse
and fold it like a stillborn child into the hole.
Your husband's oldest brother leads the ritual,
and lays heavy stones across the grave. You will not
escape. Whips are cut
from the barasá tree and are strewn
above your body
> *to control your vengeance.*

A kid is sacrificed, especially when
you die in childbirth.
Your corpse is buttered with blood.

> You and I
everything stands I refuse
nothing not a stone age we are surely

"You are beaten as your mother was beaten," she sings.
> *You are ground beneath the grinding stone,*
> *you are sorghum and stone, it isn't just me,*
> *cattle wear bells, women wear irons, you*
> *control yourself and go on*

The rattle of her voice,
the rattle of iron bracelets, of teeth
into a bowl of laughter, the rattle
of a desert snake, of shell against pelvic bone,
grain against stone. The rattle in the throat.

No   barrier.
Nothing stands between us.

As your mother was beaten.
As my mother was beaten.
No distance. No distance traveled?
Nothing stands behind us.

Who does not in this world practice slavery?
No map, no model.
Nothing stands before us.

The Hamar of Southwest Ethiopia are
not the subject.

Elegy (II)

(for Florika, 1946–1979)

"Perfect the elegiac form—you'll need it, kid,"
I can almost hear her say, that voice like a cello

in minor key, accented with slow ironies of language
from at least four different European countries

she had fled through, until she came to rest uneasily
at home here in the new world where she'd die.

But the cello was not her instrument—although toward the end
she played bass with a male jazz band, a joke

or curiosity until the audience heard
the strings like lovers strain to touch her fingers.

No, the violin had been her means of music,
Rumanian gypsy that she was, dark

greengold skin stretched like a tambourine across
the drum and cymbal bones of her percussive face.

Approximate, at least, the elegiac form,
even when bare facts, which look best in black,

describe better perhaps than poetry this full-term grief.
Nine months ago she died, in autumn, at the close

of the decade. Now, in late spring, I learn of it;
now she dies backward for me, a retrospective

from June receding, through months I thought her alive—if
I thought of her at all. It had been years

since we met, and when I saw her last she didn't
hear me call her name through traffic, but crossed

the intersection already buried in her own thoughts,
while the bus bore me away beyond her hearing.

Still, we were women of an age, though she seemed always
the elder—tall, slender, that mask of watered

silk shimmering tight across her luminous skull
so eager to show itself picked clean. Dear god, my sister,

is it fifteen years since we sat on the floor in that small room
in Judith's lower-east-side apartment, thirteen

of us, alone in the world and utterly unalike, except
for the music: women's voices, quietly telling

this one's pain, that one's humiliation, her fears,
my longings, your visions, our anger. What has died into rhetoric

lived in that room, drew its breath in terror to be born.
Not all the war-soaked battlefields of time

have seen such heroism as each woman risked
sitting on the floor in a circle, those Tuesday evenings.

Young and bitter, we wore our rage like cloaks of radiance.
Our very hems sparked energy, and we were gloved

and shod with laughter, acid laughter, wicked laughter,
armored with glee for all our dangerous plots.

/ / /

I wonder in what plot you lie now—you, who had managed
to be a myth even while alive:

each of us misremembers her own version of you.
Judith always thought you were raised Catholic,

Peggy felt you were atheist and Marxist, I could swear
I recall some story of how you had been smuggled

out of a Rumanian Jewish ghetto while
the Nazi landlords were in charge, and how

you were a child prodigy who escaped your mother
after several nervous breakdowns. We agree,

however, on certain versions of our myth about you:
how you were forced to bed five days each month

with cramps so powerful they drove you to your knees,
despite all remedies devised; you who loved

word games almost as much as the violin you'd never
touch; you, who tried to make us understand

the force of your madness—that it was not glamorous,
not always a sign of political sanity,

not when words came gagging, landscapes flattened, toothed
doorways yawned, not when the violin played

by itself. You were "the invisible woman" in my poem.
You were the first woman I heard say

that oppression's greatest sin wasn't in refusing
to grant what was due, but in refusing to accept

what the oppressed could give. How many years had you spent
in asylums, how many years more would you spend,

before and after that clearing in the jungle of your nightmares,
that sunlit space where women's voices almost

convinced you to play again? In time, we went our ways,
keeping in touch, reconstructing our lives

as best we could, making ourselves and history
alone and with other women. I saw you a few times

to really talk, we spoke by phone, then less and less.
I heard you'd moved away, back home to Europe,

then back home here, then made your home in California.
I imagined things were bad: I heard about

a break-up with a man, a new man, then another.
You were on heavy drugs. You fought, and kicked

the habit. It fought back. You wanted no sisterhood.
Rumors? Projections? Additions to the myth?

What I will live with is: we failed you utterly.
This was not our fault; we were powerless to give.

This was our fault. It was our most oh grievous fault.
The very last I knew, you, who founded

You're dead, no longer one of us. You're dead. How dare you?
Wait—walk among us, haunt us, drive us sane.

I must perfect the elegiac form, I know,
for others will die, have died, are dying now,

all our female dead, their silence louder than a violin
could drown. Was this nausea the one you felt?

Look at these lines: awkward approximations of a form,
opportunistic usage of your death.

Let it all go then, including the temptation to see you
as a martyr, or even a casualty.

You were yourself, I need not make you into Woman.
This grief is for you alone, specific, personal.

Goodbye, my dear. Close the volcanic eyes that flickered
in that lovely face. Put the violin away now.

I stand above a grave I've never seen and pray,
but not for you. "Pray for the living," you laugh.

I pray: God damn all silences except those sweat-freshened
by making love or art or revolution.

the first "women's liberation band" we called it,
you were playing stoned on smack in a male

jazz combo, gigging one-night stands at seedy joints
in Oakland or L.A.—but trying to form a women's

string quartet in the afternoons. Damn you, Florika,
listen: Prokofiev's second violin concerto

is mourning for you on the phonograph, while I
write these words, stupidly crying at the typewriter

nine months after—what? the overdose? Too late
these tears, too late these words to play with now,

too late my second-guessing at your life or death,
too late to free the years of silence—no sweet

string rejoicing under your bow, no remedy
for the "incorrect" pain of your bleeding, no answer to madness,

no sound. We die each day in silence, hush, we're dying.
We dream each night a music we've never heard,

and now I'll dream your ghostly face white-wreathed in garlic
flowers. Yours was the wild hair streaming I wrote of,

yours were the castinets you gave my newborn child
—which I still have. Their click has chipped away

the paint—orange and blue—for a decade. That click
echoes through the silence like a clock.

/ / /

1

White Sound

(for Jewell Parker Rhodes)

> "It is not right
> for mourning to enter a house of poetry."
> —Sappho

1

"Forgive me for not having heard
what your silence was saying more clearly;
I was busy calling you deaf."
—Those, the first words I wrote
on coming to this quiet place, lie
now at the bottom of the lake,
their ripples on the surface long since
stilled, the waterruffles having reached
the banks and scampered up in soundwaves
to shake themselves dry and, looking left and right,
move off toward the deeper woods.

I follow more slowly, picking my way
across ground-cover less grass than myrtle
flowering now white, now purple, between
columns of hemlock and white pine.
Each forsythia deafens with its exclusive claim
to be the burning bush: God in me! No,
me! No, God in *me!* The honeysuckle is fanatic,
a religious fundamentalist, not like the trillium,
which keeps to itself in stands of four or five,
each chaste bloom three-petaled and white
as white mint, each stem a slender green as green.

Behind me, pagan in the orchard,
apple-blossom boughs are studded with bees
who rise and settle, rise again and settle

like a pointillist lover repositioning an embrace
or like decorative hatpins tufted in yellowbrown velvet
stabbing their lace-pale cushion.

I am a city woman.

2
Metaphysician, heal thyself. Why should I
find it easier to grow impatiens on a
tarblistered roof than plant
words onto paper when there is no acid
in my soil? Ashamed of such excuses,
I watch the male cardinal smear wingspread-width
the spring sky with color red on blue fresh
from the art of Mycenaean Crete. It can be done.

Even for me, though, who give myself
airs of domesticity, these trails crunching
pleasantly underfoot feel a bit tame—
not like a seacoast eroding the heart,
or a city intersection. One day, the rain
brightens a twilight, pearling
white drops thick from a thick white sky.
I walk through its beaded curtain

wearing sensible shoes, but I am
a city woman still. I hallucinate
the telephone. I dream I have missed a train.
I dream I am paralyzed from the neck down
because of an accident in a swimming pool
in which I was hit surprisingly hard with a
plastic toy. I dream I can no longer

tell the screams of a human from those of a jay:
streetcurses, brakesqueal, sirens,
the whining of a child, the sobs of a hostile lover,
dreams of real wilderness, all muffled
as if by a white-sound machine.
I dream I am a siren singing underwater,

having lured myself to death.

3
How dare we call the scream of a jay
its natural sound simply because

we've never heard it sing? Things happen
in translation. While artists work here, the death toll

mounts in Florida, where I was born—
black bodies falling like needles

from a white pine tree. A volcano erupts.
Nothing so pacified, inert, or tame

it can be trusted beyond a certain solstice
of gratuitous pain: the well-meant joke on sex or race

the teller can afford not to hear clearly,
all honorable men counting on laughter

to drown out the crude Polack strains
of a Chopin étude. If a woman paces

in her room, black fists clenched white
with anger; if a woman works in her cabin

defying terror to understand another
woman on her page; if a woman

stalks herself on canvas; if a woman
builds herself jade burial armor;

if a woman walks in the woods and walks
and walks and grinds her white forehead

against indifferent moss and weeps
and rages at such weeping, what does it mean?

If a woman falls in the forest and
no one hears, is there sound?

4

> There is a poem missing here,
> unlike the deliberate flaw the Navajo weaver
> leaves in her blanket—to let the soul out.
> Such a poem would be a luxury, a passion;
> it could afford trust, it could have something
> to do with love, but craftily. Or
> it could be raucous with humor—
> the special kind those who have so deplorably
> lost their sense of, have, when alone
> with one another. It could be a lament,
> frangible as a bird's egg, longing to break
> the silence. But it would sing, at least,
> the way an elegy might stretch its grief taut

on a violin string, unafraid to mourn and still
be beautiful. Such poems are rare.

To be deflected from their making by pain
or powerlessness is the greatest loss.
To be deflected from their making by ignorance
or power, by choice, might be the only sin.

We settle for cheap grace too often.

5
I thought I had come to this place to stage
the mysteries as they once might have been
celebrated. I dream of having an audience
with the Three Norns—all dark-skinned women
laughing with love. I wonder
how could she have known, Demeter,
driving out of reality on the private road
in a blue car, looking older than her age.

"Remember this face"—holding out to me
a wallet photograph of a young woman, blonde, blue-
eyed. "My little girl," she says, her lips
straight as the vital-signs signal of one dead.
"She disappeared ten days ago in front of this place.
She took no clothes or anything she loved
with her, so *she* was taken, somehow. She didn't just
go, I mean." I look at her as if I have imagined her.
I say, "How old–? I mean, I'm sure she'll
come back," and I'm lying. "Fifteen," she says.
I think: Persephone, trim-ankled, gathering
flowers. "She'll come back," I say, and reach

through the rolled-down car window to touch
the bony shoulder. I shouldn't have: it brings
acidic tears to both of us. "If she's still
alive," she answers, and bites the scab on her lip.
Finally, I am silent. "I've put a tracer on her,"
she whispers, and accelerates off down the road.

Sweet god Demeter I never meant to meet you
in these woods Momma I never thought you were
still looking—for she is lost to you, lost,
whether she went willingly or was dragged,
whether she thought him attractive
or scary, whether the glitter
was in his eyes or along the edge of something
metal he pulled from his pocket. And
why ask me? Why rendezvous with me of all people
here the fool out walking in the brightening rain,
pretending I am not a city woman, not a white
woman, not a woman, just a poet?

6
Things die even if left where they belong—
which is obvious, but politics can't solve that.
Cut flowers in the city seem naturally
short-lived, but perish almost as quickly unplucked.
Already the apple-blossoms have disappeared,
the forsythia bushes gone bare green,
the trillium focusing inward to the prophesied
red berry of late summer. The lilac lavish and
are gone; narcissi, columbine, wild mustard
stand and die; the lily-of-the-valley, bridal veil,
a violet or two must tide us over until roses.

                                              / / /

I am not such a city woman I cannot celebrate
whatever I can—although the scream
that last drew me out with robe and flashlight
into the night, I knew was animal: something
trapped, devouring or being devoured.

Who said these trails were tame?
Who said however loud (or still thinks,
whispering) that genius finds itself
uncomfortable wearing certain shades of skin,
finds unreconcilable clitoris and brain
for habitation? Who welcomed mourning
into the house of poetry?

What we deny, denies us.
What we make live in art denies us
if the blood spilled to it is anyone's
but our own. All else is white sound,
drowning what we might have sung, had we
but dared to use the skill I fear as much
as you do: to recognize that we are doomed
together—human, artists, all

mad atheists insatiable for god.

The Fall of a Sparrow

> "Why can't we be friends now? . . . It's what I want. It's what
> you want." But the horses didn't want it—they swerved
> apart; the earth didn't want it, sending up rocks through
> which riders must pass single file; the temples, the tank, the
> jail, the palace, the birds, the carrion, the Guest House . . .
> they didn't want it, they said in their hundred voices, "No,
> not yet," and the sky said, "No, not there."
> —E. M. Forster, *A Passage to India*

1
To live in fear, they say,
is not to live at all. But it is
also not to die just yet.

Dustbrown, face streaked with
white, convulsively alert, the sparrow
who visits our rooftop birdhouse knows
a hunger wild as her fear.
Feathers barely soften the outline
of her armature—nerves wired
like a watchspring, shudder, blink, tick,
rupturing into flight even when nothing
threatens. She knows some eye is on her.

Such vigilance is equaled only by
the patience of one other, a perfect complement—
the patch of shadow blacker than the sootgrayed
tar, but dappled by two sunspots as twin geodes
of lightning-flecked rockcrystal might glimmer
from a mineshaft—the courtier, unruffled enemy
of this twitterclown's alarm. Oh murderous grace,
cat I have loved above all other cats, companion
of my desk and bed, tear-taster, anklet of fur
against November drafts, breath at my ear,

nip erotic at my knee, familiar of
my unremembered powers, he who bestows the rumble
of love at my first touch.

How commonplace, and how astonishing, I say,
that when the sparrow looks at all that
loveliness, she sees
a killer. He walks in beauty
like a death. Even when he sleeps
indoors, she fears him, head aswivel,
blood calling out to blood. Torn so
between, what good am I? Fool, madwoman,
hemophiliac of sentiment, I still imagine
a different way. He is such a special cat, I say,
so intelligent, so curious to learn,
decorous, gentle almost to a fault,
his survival without a keeper unassured.
Surely such a creature could make the leap
that spans the mutation of self and other;
surely it is possible, surely
this one could do it, this one who nibbles cheese and vegetables
with a cetacean smile, this one, surely.
How can he bear to manifest himself as death
to such an other?

He doesn't want to look like death, you say—
you who have sharpened long your claws
against the headwinds of what some call
nature to prove all things unnatural natural—
you, of all people, say, But it's his nature.
In fact, you say, he tries for camouflage
in his surroundings, to disguise himself so he

will look like anything but death to her. See
how pathetically he waits for her to comprehend
that really he is just a shadow, his hope
straining toward her trust?

And if *she* could make the leap, I agree,
not to erupt in flight and churn
the currents of her fear, but once, instead,
embrace her dive with full-arched wings
and glide through grace reckless as a leaf
of autumn lemniscates to meet the shade
cast by itself below; if once, I say,
in such abandon she could light, mad
as a saint, in blessing, on his head,
in proof of her imaginative power to conceive
he might be other than her death—

She'd die for it, you say. Something went wrong,
terribly wrong, on this planet, you say again.
I blink, and turn away.

2
July. Selected journal entries—and exits:

> Discarded in the gutter, a carton for a folding gate
> of wire and mesh, the kind you place at doorways and the heads
> of stairs: "Keeps Baby and Pets Contained but Happy," reads
> the text. Later, at sunset, the television mourns
>
> astonishing and commonplace news: a ten-year-old boy
> killed himself. His name was Santos.

/ / /

He had been depressed. He lived in the barrio
and died there, hanging from his size-small belt in the shower,
the one room where he could be alone a while
without arousing envy.

Our son is also ten, has his own room,
weeps for a Santos he never met. He floats
the currents of Satie's "Gymnopédies" amazing
as an aerialist when practicing his music. He has
a sparrow's nightmares, but he practices death, too,
sometimes, in games. He is trying to not lie about that.

The street poster—a former comrade's blown-up
face proclaiming himself the last pure leader,
proclaiming himself betrayed by everyone, proclaiming
the catastrophes to come with joy so fearful
it smears the print: world famine and world war,
carnage, destruction, blood, apocalypse. "The hatred
that already burns in the hearts of millions is
going to spread and deepen," he exults, "so let's go
out and let's not only die—"
        —but let's live? I ask aloud—
"—but let's kill to make revolution."
This month, in this state, two thirteen-year-old
boys are standing trial for murder. At that age,
in the faith I left behind, they proclaim a boy a man.
Today, a new strong man outlawed all music
from his revolution, having already excluded women.

                                    / / /

3
Not to simplify, not to, not to.
Women can also kill, can kill, can kill.
Forget me not let me not let me not fear.

The singsong twitter of the daft,
the lullaby of the long sleep,
the chant of a novice, the left-hand
sostenuto, the voluntary purr.
    I can do it I can do it I can do it.
The little brain that tried.

Can the mad sin?
No. They have cast their sin outside themselves
and that has made them mad.

Can the mad sin?
No. They are already damned.

Can the mad sin?
No. Sin requires choice.
Choice requires sanity.

Can the mad sin?
No. Both sanity and sin require choice.
They have chosen not to choose.

Can the mad sin?
No. It is (not) their nature.

Can the mad sin?
No. They have fallen into grace
on full-arched wings.

/ / /

Can the mad sin?
Yes. I have fallen from grace, a leaf crisped
from the tree. I have fallen from grace
because the sin, which was my death, was beautiful.

4
I chose. I chose a different way. In proof
of lost imaginative powers, I did not choose
security, the sanitized brain, the heart content
with scraps from my cave-fire. I did not marry
Edgar Linton or even Tom Buchanan.
Heathcliff would be my husband, I would save
Gatsby for living greatness. I would make the leap
that was not in your nature or my own,
practicing not to die even at the price
of training the heart to love in fear,
a terror wild as hunger but as holy.
Surely I could do it. Surely
        —forget me not to simplify can kill—
you could. This time, on this planet even,
surely, yes, you said, hope straining toward my trust.

> Ding dong something wrong
> chime each season's chill
> time and treason will
> rhyme or reason kill

Can the mad sin?
Yes, oh yes:

For I myself have blinded both the doors
through which love might have entered
wearing any camouflage not yours.

5
Duel in the sun or the shadow,
it ends the same.
She rides on her revenge for days
to his desert hideaway. She fires
the signal shot. He shouts a welcome.
She aims at him, shoots, hits. He falls.
She screams his name and drops her weapons.
He struggles upright, aims, shoots her, and hits.
She falls. He screams her name.
How shocked each lover is to hit the mark aimed for.
How they crawl toward one another between
bullets, how they weep and curse and call
each other liars, how they bleed their parts
according to the rules.

I've heard your promises before, she rails.
How could you do this to me, he recites.
I'm dying, he calls, see, I'm a shadow now, come to me, hurry.
You lie, she sings, it's in your nature,
I was a fool. She claws the rockface, scaling
her own jagged hunger. Red lacy cuffs unfeather
from both her wrists. She climbs,
she reaches him, leaf dizzying upward in her
inner hurricane's blind eye.
"I love you," he sobs. At last and means it.
Kisses her and dies. One gesture
later—her hand poised on his head in blessing—

she is dead as well.
High on a ledge above sunset and cliché
their bodies cling. Oh beauteous enemy.
Oh murderous grace, inevitable.

6
Until now, I'd have ended there. And been grateful.
(Transcendence, even "not at the last but
at the very last" still worth damnation.)
But this once I find myself
turn, imagining how to imagine
a way to descend and still live. This time,
am I done with deathbed reunions made possible
because only then we forgive one another
our individual means of survival?

Surely, this time, I am done with professions of love
between taking aim, surely done with
the beauty of sin, dying, death. Oh let me be
done with all revolutions that long for
catastrophe, done with this crawling
along the rockface, with training
my heart to live in love, killing for it,
coming undone.

Surely this time I will gather my wits, doggerel,
props, and exit this tragedy, knowing that some will say
this proves I lack tragic sense—but knowing the oldest
of tragediennes is always some terrified clown
circling a doom she insists is comedic,
and knowing as well how preposterous
I must look now, and how commonplace:

blind, bloody, convulsively alert, face streaked
with autumn, ridiculously
twittering I can do it rhyme and reason
I can do it, see?

Now, at the last, of course, something will
happen naturally not in our natures. It could be
anything except imagined until it appears—
only recognized then as then only inevitable.
Something to rupture even the best-trained heart
into dreading love possible: something all over
rock, beak, fang, right-hand melody,
something constraining again as a gate
meshed from nervewire—lost, dreamt, and familiar.

Then the eye burns as if it could see.
Then one of us says, Why can't we
love now? It's what I want. It's what you want.

But our shadows don't want it—they fade with the light;
the earth doesn't want it, sending up rocks
through which lovers must crawl single file;
the gutters, the roofs, the games, the asylums,
the leaves, the famished, the birdhouse . . . they
don't want it, they say in their hundred voices,
No, not yet, and the planet repeats, *No, not here.*

The Hallowing of Hell
A PSALM IN NINE CIRCLES

> "Why, this is hell, nor are we out of it."
> —Marlowe's *Doctor Faustus*

1
The Rider is stationary
in Einstein's democratic universe;
all objects rush past her.
What rushes toward
wears bluish light: high frequency and energy.
What rushes away
wears reddish light: low frequency, low energy.
We each observe the same
laws of physics, but every individual
view is relative, despite all mass and energy
being in fact equivalent.
Material falling toward a Black Hole would liberate
tremendous energy just before vanishing into it.
Black Holes, in turn, release enormous energy
by swallowing stars.
"All of astrophysics," the scientist says,
"is about nature's attempt to free the energy in matter."
The impossible must happen.
The Rider moves.

(Stay in motion.)

2
You have gained the Self.
Sunset slanting through a glass of burgundy,
a sparrow wading in the fountain,
a dead man on the phonograph singing
a lullaby to his son.
A dead woman's villanelle
about practicing loss.
Your mother's hands, attached

to your wrists now, lying in your lap;
your son's hands, in a distant room,
practicing the Bach "Solfegietto" you played
long ago. Enemies insisting god exists
and friends proclaiming there's no god.
You are losing the Mother,
you may yet lose the Husband,
you have lost the Sister,
you will lose the Child,
all in the nature of things.
But you have gained the Self.

Everything *seems.* The sun,
for example, is a globe of burgundy glass.
What profiteth it you
to lose the whole world if
you gain your own soul?

                              (*Try, at least try.*)

3
Let us say
she is still unfashionably metaphysical,
hopelessly so, unsalvageable, damned.
Let us admit that she has abused
this dubious gift, herself, on occasion—
not only cynically to deny it, but
worse: to use it as escape, abstraction,
ectoplasm to wisp away the sacred Specific
(though not the political). Now
she still tries all broken bitter to bless
each thing with magical properties,

to see mystery where no mystery exists,
embarrassing good people who believe
that once you look deeply enough
into the eyes of suffering you
can see nothing else again.

Life have mercy upon us.
Death have mercy upon us.
Life have mercy upon us.

Let us try.

> (*Start with whatever your glance first falls on.*)

4
The flowers on my desk
are lilies: lemon lilies,
Peruvian lilies, and *gloriosa.*
Praise be to real things, simple, lowly,
praise be the words to name them.
Praise be to Phosphor, our larkspur Siamese,
in her circle of sleep under the desk lamp.
Praise be to paper and ink, pencil and typewriter.
Praise be to the city beyond my window, stirring
into dawn, praise to the lemonlily-colored
orange juice in my glazed pottery cup,
the books ranged like armies of unalterable light
along my shelves; praise be to those, alive or dead,
who wrote them, those who published them,
who printed, bound, sold, bought them,
who gave them to others, and who read them.

/ / /

Blessed be the existence of the possibility of
poetry. Blessed be the flowers on my desk.

(*A beginning. Now. Again.*)

5
And blessed be the women who get you through:
the woman who lets you stay in her apartment,
the woman who takes you out for a drink,
the woman who guides you through the House of Mirrors
    in Copenhagen's Tivoli,
the woman who walks you through the Belvedere
    gardens of maroon-stalked orange gladioli,
the woman who loans you money,
the woman who has fresh Kleenex,
the woman who offers to chart your horoscope,
the woman who writes a stranger a letter about her poems,
the woman who sells your jewelry for you,
the woman who feeds your cats when you're gone,
the woman who makes you laugh,
the woman who tempts you to a superficial movie,
the woman who sees through Aquinas,
the woman who gives you a ream of 20-pound bond paper,
the woman who always seems to have an extra concert ticket,
the woman who prays for you,
the woman who writes her own books,
the woman who insists you keep a set of her keys,
the woman who gets you a poetry reading,
the woman who rings up to see how it's going,
the woman who loans you a book,
the woman who loves a man and is going through the same thing,
the woman who loves a woman and is going through the same thing,
the woman who gives you an inflatable travel pillow,

the woman you can show a first draft to,
the woman who cries with you,
the woman who makes you eat something,
the woman who gives you work to do,
the woman who reminds you to be fair,
the woman who helps you face answering letters,
the woman who talks about light,
the woman who falls in love with you
        but remains your friend,
the woman you yourself once loved above all women—
        weaned before her time, who hates you for that
        weaning now—blessed be her freeing vengeance even;
blessed be all the love like waves of light
        of all the others.
Blessed, blessed be the women who get you through.

(*Good. Again now, again.*)

6
To build a heaven in hell's despite
is not so necessary, given such a world.
Once, snorkeling in Paraíso Reef off Mexico,
we entered an innocent universe, if not
a democratic one. Black coral,
fiery feather stars, sea lilies waltzed
along the current, and the fish called
Shy Squirrels played between our outstretched fingers.
A Queen Angelfish, prism-iridescent,
made her dowager's progress past spiny sea urchins.
The only sound was my own breathing—and a Yellow Grunt
sucking calmly on algae, the only light
that which refracted through water in patterns duned
like stretchmarks on a pregnant woman's belly,

a splendor of design. That light rushed
neither toward you nor away from you; it swayed
around you, bathed you, it became the water.
I swam through it, weightless as a swallowed star
moves, moving, moved. In such a world,
the task is less to build
than excavate a heaven in hell's despair.

                    (*Better and better. Now, again.*)

7
So blessed be the child you call your son;
may his paths be lit with grace.
Blessed be his understanding,
the wisdom he almost knows he already has.
Blessed be his piano keys and clarinet keys
and lost skatekeys and doorkeys.
Blessed be his grief for battered children
and for baby seals and the great whales, blessed
his love of Shakespeare and snowballs.
Blessed be his magic spells and home runs,
his dungeons, his dragons, his Debussy, his dolls,
blessed be his wit's edge and his compassionate heart,
blessed be his friends and phone calls and the first
leaves of his sexual budding.
Blessed be his sense of justice, his anger
and defense of his own rights.
Blessed be his rebellion against you.
Blessed be the boy you call your son.

                    (*Here it is. Try. Again. Again.*)

                                              / / /

8

And blessed be the man I've lived with almost twenty years.
Blessed be this past year of unspontaneous combustion.
Blessed be our two dead selves who died that year;
may they rest in peace.
Blessed be the dogged, furious, insistent
capability of change.
Blessed be his eyes, dark never except with pain,
but mostly the color of sunlight glimpsed looking up
from under the sea surface—a bluish light,
high frequency, that rushes toward you.
Blessed be his just anger, blessed
all his lightbulbs changed and garbage taken out,
his mislaid pliers and lost wallets,
blessed be the blood-jet of *his* poetry,
blessed be the friends who get him through,
blessed be his scratched Keith Jarrett and Scriabin records,
blessed be his fuchsia flowers and his precious
jacaranda tree, blessed be
the kiss we shared in an open field, thunderstorm-soaked
among the ruins of Mayan sacrifice.
Blessed be the sight of him underwater, each
of us beckoning, watching through respective masks
and smiling above teeth clenched on our own oxygen.
Blessed be his fear of the living god
in himself, and his love of that. Blessed
be his face, laughing, between my laughing knees
one August afternoon, blessed be
all the moments-into-years with him—
including the terror, the despair, the mutual
cruelties and cowardices.
Blessed be the years to come, together or apart,

for something in each of us is eternally
equivalent, matter and energy, to something
in the other. Blessed be his courage and his genius,
his Tarot deck and Buddhist beads, his love
of men and his disowning masculinity.
Blessed be life with him and without him,
blessed be the utterly new questions broken open now
and blessed be the lack of tidy answers.
Blessed be the man I'll love in some way till I die.

(*Yes yes again yes again again yes*)

9
Blessed be the hands that dare write this.
Blessed be even my failures, hypocrisies, self-
sustained martyrdoms—blessed be their recognition.
Blessed be the child I was; I gather her
and all her discrete pain into my arms.
Blessed be the crochety, eccentric, and terrific
raucous wise old woman I intend to be; I gather
her decaying matter into my arms.
Blessed be all my fears and the losing of them,
all my loves and the losing of them,
all my lives and the losing of them;
blessed be the rose light they recede in.
Blessed be whatever comes, floating
in a luminescence blue and inevitable as the sea.
Blessed be this continual unrelenting constant gradual
hallowing of hell, of everything I know
and everything I meet for the first time,
this great work of living.
Blessed be the energy of dark stars and the light

of long-dead suns, the ongoing task
to see as holy, to make holy
every specific particle one can imagine, the imagination
holy. Blessed be the heights and the depths.
Blessed be change—and its sense of humor.
Blessed be survival—and its sense of honor.
Blessed be death—and its sense of relief.
Blessed be life—and its sense.
Blessed be the eyes that dare read this.

> Hosanna in the highest
> Hosanna in the lowest
>
> As it was never before,
> is not now and yet shall be,
> worlds without end

> *Again*

Poems

1 9 8 2 – 1 9 8 8

The Exiles

(for Isel Rivero)

Where you had wandered, jagged footprints
pressed like kisses, unfelt, bleeding mutely
across another road of broken glass;

where you had wandered, mad girl, singing
to yourself, indifferent others, or no one, as if
the act—to sing at all—invented song;

where you had wandered, bitter laughter
checked for an hour in a cathedral vestibule, despair
parked for an evening outside glad-lit party windows;

where you had wandered, alchemizing love,
defining, redefining it, unearthing it,
inventing and invoking, waiting, moving on;

on from the new world, careless and greedy
in its hunger, its ways of desire; illiterate
at its loving; starved eyes too wide, starved bodies

too swollen, too famished to be wise in love;
backward toward cities with windows leaded
like half-lidded eyes, cities which had seen too many

lovers' conquests, warriors' conquests,
bodies sleek and surfeited that had forgotten appetite,
a world past hoping, elegant in its despair.

Where you had wandered, grey dawns and midnights
streetlamp-punctured, chilled rosé twilights never warmed
by a childhood-pungent jasmine tree;

where you had wandered, homelessly at home
in the labor of it, cherishing the color blue
when it could be spotted: in a violet, in an eye;

where you had wandered brought you, eventual, inevitable,
doomed, blessed, cursed, destined, to where I
crouched hiding: nothing cerulean about me,

nothing azure, only eyes dark, starved, peering
through walls paned in cracked glass, my handprints
carnadine as kisses unspent. I beckoned,

warning you away. You saw another mad girl
inventing song, hope, love, bitter laughter.
You saw in the bloody handprints on the pane

violet rose windows of stained glass.
And you struck like a great bell
through my silences, a Matins shattering the night,

a pendulum of sound I climbed
until it filled all motion, swinging, welled all words.
The shards of my life were melting back to sand.

And all these jasmine-redolent rosé twilights later,
I remember not believing the face transformed by love
your lens had captured could be mine.

And all this tearing and these tears
inflicted on the hapless liberating angel
by the captive you set free, track me

where I wander, jagged footprints
pressed like careless, greedy kisses
on the broken, sharp-edged, glittering air.

Except that you, like a bloodsource tolling its pulse
to clot each artery I sever, peal,
Angelus from the ravaged belltower of the heart,

a sweet relentless summoning unfurled
to haunt the jasmine air. It calls
the weary children in from play among blue shadows.

It tolls your name through veins
of wrist and throat. It tolls for thee and me—
as if it could still toll us home.

Van Gogh at Saint-Rémy and Arles

(for Karen Berry)

"Ignore the obvious:
exaggerate the essential."
—Vincent Van Gogh, *Dear Theo*

Obvious that this is the final year:
but it is the present year.

Obvious the asylum walls:
but they enclose a garden.

Obvious the severed ear:
but now the babble is stilled.

Obvious the bars on the window:
but cypresses exuberate beyond them.

Obvious the whining mistral wind:
but then the hush of rain.

Obvious the grape-blue shadows, looming mountains:
but that one bush now, flowering white.

Obvious that only seventy days remain:
but seventy canvases wait primed.

Obvious this luxuriance of farmfields:
essential, their geometry.

Obvious the details:
essential, the perspective.

Obvious the writhing of mad olive trees:
essential, the single arc of almond branch in bud.

/ / /

The explosion under the heart, oh obvious.
But this, the rising,
hemorrhaging colour, staggering
homeward thought to be drunk, to where light
spreads like a runner on the narrow stairs up
to the narrow bed: dark radiance, the deliberate act.

Obvious, crows over a wheatfield at the last.
But this, essential, at the very last: sundrenched wheatsheaves
slouching serene as angels in a gleaned field—
a commonplace harvest, luminous, reaped.

Two Women

Never the rosebud nor the rain, my dear,
were you to me.
Never the sunset nor the dawn
was I to you.
Indulgences of indolent linguistics
have no place between two women such as we,
two women of a temperament more prone
to cactus thorns and blizzards,
two women living in an age
of instant fissioned noon before
an everlasting night.

Never the gifts of time and space, my dear,
the luxuries of dailiness that grace most lovers' lives
lifelong (and so become ignored):
a quiet cup of tea shared
on an autumn afternoon before the fire,
desultory conversations about nothing in particular—
a shutter that needs fixing soon, or whether
it might snow tomorrow;
what to have for dinner and who feels like cooking;
and Have you seen my glasses No Now where
can I have put them this time
or Do check the doctor for that coughing, love,
alright alright I didn't mean to nag.

Never the simple pleasures: lusty quarrels
and lustier reconciliations, certainty,
comfortable boredom in forgetting
for whole days that the beloved actually exists—
that particular liberty more perilous
than an enslavement.

/ / /

None of these common joys were ours.
By chance, choice, character, and challenge,
we endured enjoying a shared century and gender
and our own separate, identical, and polar souls.
So when I looked at you I never saw
a rosebud or the rain,
and when you looked at me you never thought
of sunset or of dawn.

Something else woke to breathe along our gaze,
ancient and ageless—
so heavy with grief that only
those two pairs of eyes could have borne it,
so airy with laughter that only
those two pairs of lips could have anchored it,
so fearful with recognition that only
those two hearts' audacities could have attempted it.

For when I looked at you I saw
        the woman who discovered fire.
And when you looked at me you saw
        the woman who domesticated animals.

For you were the midwife inventing her skills
and I was the weaver who built the first loom.

You were the sacrifice on the Aztec altar,
I was the witch aflame with my dying.

You were the queen abdicating your throne,
I was the warrior who despised killing.

/ / /

You were the peasant gathering firewood,
I was the courtesan hoarding poisons.

You were the fugitive from father and brothers,
I was the recluse giving you shelter.

You were the priestess blessing the grain,
I was the abbess teaching my novices.

You were the raped slave longing for death,
I was the battered wife with nowhere to go.

You were the acrobat vaulting through hoops,
I was the aerialist tense on my wire.

You were the matron who let me escape,
I was the captive who stopped to look back.

You were the clitoridectomized maiden,
I was the child with three-inch bound feet.

You were the scientist scanning your microscope,
I was the sculptor caressing my marble.

You, the guerrilla cradling your rifle,
I, the bar-girl hiding my infant;
you, the prisoner electrode-interrogated,
I, the patient electrode-treated.

We were the women who huddled in rags
for the bitter warmth of each other,
who had given and given and sickened and died.

/ / /

You were the woman dead of abortion,
I was the woman dead in childbirth.

You were the actress who drank too much,
I was the housewife who swallowed pills.

You were the orphan who raised yourself,
I was the bastard who named myself.

You were the woman who had no style,
I was the woman phobic with fear.

We were the women who mourned through our cells,
bone-raw, blood-raw, who had found and then lost
and then found one another again.

You were the woman who dared write new laws,
I was the woman who dared learn to read.

You were the woman who risked loving women,
I was the woman who tried to love men.

We were the women who tested our strengths
for the play of it—gladiators
for no one's amusement
but that of our own—oiled body to body,
knife mind against mind.

You were the woman who sang in the forest,
I was the woman who danced by the sea.

We were the women who dared to say No.

/ / /

We were the women who fought back, left clues,
passed it along, hoped
for some time to ourselves.

We were the women we feared and desired.

These were the joys we were cursed with, the griefs
we were blessed with, my darling.
These were the revenants awake in our gaze,
resurrected, claiming the love of two cynical innocents
as the medium for their rebellion.
These were the faceted energies strung on the glances
we flung round each other, the only possessions
adorning our radiant nakedness.

And what we possessed, possessed us—
though possession was hardly the point.

Desire was the point—
for food, water, shelter, peace.
Hunger for freedom, the bread of the body.
Thirst after laughter, the wine of the soul.
All of these famishments
gnawed in my hunger for you,
parched through your thirsting for me.

We were two women who saw
we could save the whole world,
and ourselves, but never
each other,

two women who knew how to plot,
how to meet
how to part,
how to wait,

two women commuting the planet
to celebrate passion
in a terminal epoch.

And yes, at a time of apocalypse, we were two women
who stole dawns and sunsets
to lie in each other's arms, touching
bright thorns of suffering through blizzards of tears.

But touching as well
    —carry it through, risk it, dare the defiance
    of every convention, even of metaphor—
touching yes petals of flesh damp as wild rosebuds yes
drenched by spring rain.

The Mirror Painter

(Among the most treasured appointments in eighteenth-century
European homes of wealth and culture were Chinese mirror paintings.
Thought to have been a translation of the European tradition of
mirror-glass decoration, the Chinese works developed far beyond
that original conceit, believed to have been introduced into China
by seventeenth-century Jesuit missionaries. Chinese artisans first
removed the silvering from the back of the mirror in those areas they
intended to paint; they then painted the panel-back in reverse, so that
the image would be perfectly formed when viewed from the front. In
the earlier works, broad expanses of silver were retained to preserve the
reflectivity of the glass. Later, only enough of the mirrored surface was
reserved for subtle highlights—for example, the current of a painted
river with silver wave crests.)

From the first, she refused to settle
for mere reflection or passive canvas.
For the invention of a public self
a blend of art and artifice would be required,
disclosure with discretion, contrarily
discovered as organic only once
the work was whole.

She staked all on the assumption
that a viewer, shocked by familiar features' sudden
luminosity, would recognize herself.
She had not imagined this would alter
perceiver or perceived, and yet
the form enthralled her; such freedom,
she reasoned, might become contagious.

More hands might then collaborate, redefine

old and invent new powers—a masterpiece unique
in style, tone, subject, lucency, inviting
more reflection, in time illumining
even those who'd never been permitted
to approach themselves.
She foresaw every danger except one.

She had not expected her private struggle
to be seen as quaint, had not anticipated
becoming fashionable, collectable,
dinner-party gossip. They could not endure
untrivialized, she finally understood,
such broad expanses of reflection.
But neither could they avert their eyes.

Gradually, with some pain, she reduced the shining
spaces one by one, tears glimmering to watch the silver
peel away, flakes of light lost from embrittled glass.
Pigmented creatures grazed now in their place—
alizarin chimeras beside common heifers; dazzle-flecked
salmon struggled upstream to lay their orchid eggs in eagles'
aeries; a naked shepherdess danced on a precipice.

Bosch hells rose livid in Brueghel villages
and rollicked with despair. Here and there,
radiance still sought reflection: a ghostly lunar
smile, windows burnished in a ruined tower, the sheen
of a baboon's behind, the surprise glazed
on a dying warrior's grin. This, she was certain,
they could not misconstrue.

/ / /

They approved the new conceit, thought it provocative,
unlike her; quite amusing, to spy one's flickering self
in a tail, catch a lover's face distorted in a tankard
upended at a village brawl. Ruthless, she struck
more iridescence from her task. Trapped behind the glass,
herself a fantastic beast, she stripped whatever they might value
and abuse as precious from the surface.

She melted it, scraped, chipped it. Ankle-deep
in curls of shimmer, she shaved the glass near bald,
fingers stained with flaying brilliance, hands scarred
from too much handling of vitreosity. Nights through, alone,
she slashed her colours at the transparent obstacle
and broke, began again, again broke, and again began.
The ore of hope in her was veined too deeply.

At the next opening, what they saw surprised them.
Blood rivers boiled along banks now polluted with dismembered
limbs: a woman's hacked-off breast, the crushed leg
of a gazelle, heads severed and still screaming as they grew—
glossy, overripe fruit—from trees aflame like rooted torches.
And yet, there was a lustre glistening still
along a shredded wing that once had arched in air.

A new sensation, they exclaimed, fiery and perverse.
A delicious controversy; they could take sides. Some discussed
quietly whether such work ought to be displayed right out
in the open where anyone could see it. Some said she'd lost
her talent, sense of proportion, mind. Others conceded
a charisma in her darkening vision, a bracing lack
of lyricism, a lamentably overdue sophistication.

/ / /

Her adaptations all adopted, she planned one final work.
Years dimmed while she stayed cloistered.
It was said she'd given up, retired, gone under, broken down,
come over, come across. It was agreed no one could mix such colours
of grief and longing and still create. It was regretted
she had not fulfilled her promise, had been a minor irritant,
a minor artist. Then she announced her final exhibition.

The crowd assembled for the unveiling glimpsed briefly
one creation. It was void of all things human. Only
the landscape swelled, sloped, braided like sleeping lovers.
Burnt orange grass stubbled in no breeze. Nothing lived, moved,
sang, suffered, or could die. A cloud hung at the composition's
edge. The crowd saw only space gleaming in reflection in the one
moment before two practiced wrists burst from behind the surface.

The work lay shattered in a thousand fragments.
The artist disappeared and was not seen again.
Retrospectives and analyses still flourish: some claim
new works by unknowns bear her influence; most define
the mystery of her style as inconsistent, each period differed so.
No one has noticed the silver splinter lying still
in a dusty corner of what was once her exhibition hall.

> Look in that glass, beloved, if you would find
> the woman I am, the woman you are, entwined.

The Heart Balloon

Despite the surrounding atmosphere
being "the most inhospitable on earth"
(the television documentary tells us) micro-organisms
never visible to the naked eye
live for millennia inside solid rock
encased in ice, there, in Antarctica.

Dormant, they wake each year
for five days only—Antarctican summer—
to find themselves enclosed alive.

Fragile, improbable, miraculous,
they propagate themselves in these
five days; they age, mature, fall back
to dormancy, and sleep until they die
within the sleep within the rock
within the ice within Antarctica.

And in that sleep who knows
what dreams may come of being
again alive?
For this? you ask, Why bother
to exist at all, for this?
What mindless desperate helpless drive
insists through them on living?

Despite the surrounding atmosphere,
a grey Thanksgiving morning one November
(the documentary of memory tells me), two women
waking in a bed of love astonished
see outside the window a crimson, perfect
heart mid-air above the city street,

fragile, miraculous, within
the granite air within rock-towered canyons
within the sleeping city.

One of the women whispers, We
must rescue it. She flings on sweater, jeans, boots,
to fly downstairs, out to the street, chasing
the heart balloon, chasing the wind it rides, dodging
the traffic, straining for its improbable perfection just
out of reach. A rebel shift of wind,
unlikely as five summer days preserved in ice,
breathes it within her arms.

The other woman, watching
from the window, cheers her on. Back
through the rock, back, back up the stairs, back
to their bed she bears it, lightly, in her hands.
For this? you ask, Why
bother to rise at all, the helium heart,
to hover against the ceiling's limits
leaking a love not visible to the naked eye
while two women stare at it in wonder?

Is the heart then a micro-organism
as well as a balloon of passing buoyancy,
improbably alive
in a surrounding atmosphere
the most inhospitable on earth?

For this? Only to be punctured, burst, and shredded,
frozen, thawed, refrozen, studded
by shards of ice until what breathes inside

the skin redensifies to liquid? To wither,
shrink, drift, deliquesce, descend
to dormancy, dream of having been alive?
To wake for five days only
and spangle itself mid-air, improbable?
You call the question up
through layered millennia of ice and rock:
For this? To let the mindless desperate helpless drive
insist through us on living?

This is Antarctica, nor are we out of it.

Rocks
(the documentary tells us)
preserve
within
themselves
our best,
our oldest,
and our ultimate
history.

Geography Lesson

Your place is the land of fire under water,
cobalt rocks pillowed on ochre, pewter plumes
of steam tossed high, incessant, up from delphic hollows;
a place where light uncurdled spills
fresh-milked from the mist, feathering each hill's silhouette,
churning each waterfall, to pool at last in tidal crevices
along the shorelines of your eyes.

My place is the city, heart of the human heart,
the *polis,* the poème concrète, where anguish paces at a speed
swifter than rapids, where every day's loud torment knocks
at each midnight's unsilent terror; a place where the dark glare
of unnatural light for one breath only holds suspended
peace when sunset stains the wheeling gull, wings sooted, poised
above a sea of glassy towers, to cry out in my voice.

Your place is an island region, where earth's breath still
is visible exhaling geysers: where mountains still express
their meaning, hot-tongued in lavic languages; where
the wanton coast beaches herself, lilaceous, lapis, indigo sands
spread amorous for the azurous lapping of the waves.
Viridescence there uncurls its fronds unhurried
in bell-flowers amber-languid as your hair.

My place is an island city, where the breath stands still
in steel-ribbed lungs to watch one palette of slate grey
shift through a subtle repertoire. Love here waits
slit-skirted under every streetlamp, screams at too many
children in too small a room, sits empty-eyed in traffic,
lies talking to herself in doorways, laughs too readily
at hatred's humour, writes poetry at three A.M.

/ / /

And yet, you now rage restless through your native splendour,
homeless and harried, misunderstanding how misunderstood
you are there, effectively impolitic, solitary, rarely alone.
And yet, I now grow roses on a tarslick roof; clematis
climbs my wisteria; jasmine and watercress, rosemary, mint
insist their sharp perfumes toward where I choose to sit, alone.
Both forged in irony, each does the best she can.

Nothing lasts longer than it must. Shorelines erode,
plains crack and blister into mountains, mountains dwindle
hillward, and cities surely crumble faster in the fall of time
than a fuchsia plant drops careless amethyst blooms. Love, too,
survives when and where possible—dazzling this glance, singing
along that voice, braiding locks of hair through strands of poetry.
Heart of the human heart, the fire under water, Love springs

gratuitous weeds defiantly in granite, lends words
to what you thought unutterable. Homeless, nurturant,
harried, insistent, Love strides unrecognized through crowds
and sits secluded as an island. Love is the visitor no place
can root or cultivate deliberately, the edifice no one constructs
or renovates by plan, the irony that can descend like grace
soot-winged, the undecipherable delphic oracle. Listen

where Love tolls the petals for us, each peal rung
and rung and wrung again, until the sentence in its full enormity
is both pronounced and comprehended: Hold fast to what you know
and also do not know. The worst will pass, the best will fade.
Others may swarm across continents or cling, peninsulan,
to safety. But each of you is still an island woman. Defiant, each
has refused to learn—and never now will know—her proper place.

The Mad Girl's Song

Madness, to trust like this;
madness, to tell you so.
Madness, to suffocate with Yes
what gasping whispers No.

Madness, to feel so glad.
Madness, to be so free.
Madness, to have thought me mad
for having tried to flee.

I had been sane so long,
I had been cautious and wise.
I had slept the sober sleep of the strong
and dreamed of the ways love dies.

Madness, to glance your way;
madness, to stop and stare.
Madness, to run toward a storm to play
with the lightning's pretty flare.

Madness, to speak your name.
Madness, to flirt with dread.
I, who could safely claim
to be serene and dead,

who knew better than to wake
and believe the world was new.
Madness, to rise and walk,
and madness to walk towards you.

You are too much like me,
familiar and unknown,

too shrewd to ever say
my madness is mine alone.

Madness, to sing aloud.
Madness, to ever show
pride in no longer being proud,
and madness to let you know.

Turn, wrench the brain away.
Think of another's charms.
Pour a drink. Take a pill. Work. Pray.
Lie in another's arms.

Rage that the brain returns,
moth to the flame, steel
to the magnet. Rage that the body burns
with the heart's live coal, empyreal.

Madness, to sleep—when I can sleep—
merely to dream I rest with you.
Madness, the mind's first waking leap
towards you, of you, to you.

We are too much the same
to tread this deadly dance.
Madness, to lose all shame,
abandon vigilance.

I am too old to rave
lunatic, crazed, obsessed.
I am too young to brave
what all my years only guessed.

/ / /

Where is the friend who will lock me safe
away from your eyes, these thoughts, this choice?
Where is the friend who can strike me deaf
to the lyre in your voice?

You are too young to regret
drifts of decades as sand.
You are too old to forget
scars still livid from love's demand.

We are too similar, too diverse
(madness to feel such joy)
to not notice, register, seize, reverse
each advance, retreat, thrust, parry, ploy.

We are too different, too alike
(madness to think such madness double)
not to remember, wait, spring, strike
precise at the spot most vulnerable.

Madness, to have known so well
how futile this is, yet have permitted
my own deliberate ascent into hell,
voluntarily committed.

Let love numb me insensate, mercifully slain,
before the dawn of that dull vast pain
breaks when, with your help, I am once again
lucid, betrayed, struck sane.

Lithographers

Lithography, the gallery program states,
is based on the mutual antipathy
of grease and water.

>We paced another rainy afternoon
>slow in this my autumn
>elsewhere on our planet
>someone's spring, our footsteps
>echoing museum marble corridors.

>Mostly women, motionless, gazed back
>at us, two women strolling past them
>where their images hung, printed, framed:
>a woman bathing, a woman sleeping,
>a woman waking tousled after love,

>a woman dancing, two women dancing
>together, a woman with green-lidded eyes
>waiting under a streetlamp, a woman
>singing soundlessly, a woman smiling at a man
>but looking away, a woman doing up her hair.

The stone will not retain its image
unless its surface structure has been changed.

>Acid, for this, is necessary,
>the program cautions, so that the surface will accept
>the image only where it is intended.
>The stone is indiscriminate, like love.
>It must be drenched and drenched again

to forestall the natural inclination
of the surface which otherwise would welcome
any and all impressions—those hinted,
those never meant for permanence, and those
deliberately impressed to last, etched into stone.

This is the work of loving (I did not
say aloud), to drench and drench again
and etch itself in acid, to forestall
the natural inclination of our surfaces
until the structure that we are is changed.

The artist alters, embellishes, or simply
continues to build the composition, the program warns.

This is the skill of loving (I did not
name aloud), the process—lonely, patient,
taking, as they say, great pains
toward the perfecting, making *trial proofs,*
experimental proofs, progressive proofs . . .

The stone must be run through a press
under considerable pressure.

This is the weight of loving (I did not
cry aloud), the flattening crush of its imprint
intaglio beyond one's surfaces, transfiguring
pores of stone past welcome or resistance,
bearing down the burden of its message

terrifying as an annunciation, until
the simplest elements, like grease and water, combine

with vitriol, seethe back against the pressure,
billow sudden azure silk out
from the dancer's scarves, execute a woman

waking tousled after love, two women
dancing together. And if the artist risks
stone-calloused fingers, acid-splattered eyes
(I did not ask aloud), who is to judge
it was not worth the hazarding?

Perhaps you noticed
(for I could not point it out)
the small sign to remind us:

*Only a limited number of such prints
are ever possible.*

The Lost Season

Summer we never had, my love, together.
Winter we had, and autumns, and mostly springs.
Summer we never had but once—
and that the first, the only, and the last.

There was the first spring
when life might have uttered us
because you dared to sing and yet I dared not dance.

There was the later spring, the recognition,
a green fire raging like sap along the veins,
time and space turned inside out for us
so we could wear each other in great gaudy
celebration intoxicating as heady early lily
of the valley, fitting together as if cut
from a single moment of creation,
the synchronized word, double-sourced, flowing
as one at once to every sea.

Still later, there was the spring
we rearranged all of the temporary rooms
we passed through:
        There, this can be our table;
        Here, these wild daisies, bluebells, honeysuckle
        in a paper cup can be our centerpiece;
        There, my paragraph is ready, is yours
        completed, and Can our manifesto heal the world?
We walked that spring for just an hour
along another shore beside another sea.

This now, today, this is the spring
of being brave and comely, running

through streets as if too late for something,
trying to be friends trying
to make it easier trying. This is the spring
when poems fall from me like late-frosted buds,
rent garments of a mourner who does her best to laugh,
the spring when you cry suddenly as if
for no good reason, while doing your best to smile,
the spring when what we might yet say ripples beneath
unthawed sheets of silence to no sea.

Earlier autumns before this springtime chill
had waxed their coppery heat as though
each were the first and final flaming.

There was the autumn when vagabond met wanderer
in momentary shelters, each groping
through the dark for the cave-fire safe
in the other's eyes.

Later, in still another fall, there seemed
a hope of seasons turning us
along a wheel of years, a giddy steady
sweetness, a rhythmic seasoning of you and I
into the women for all seasons
we might have hazarded becoming,
a daily bread. That year the woodfire
dried us from the colder rain to come,
late-season gourds steamed their pungency across a table
lined with friends' contentment; that year
a common joy exhaled us, illumined even
filmscreens, flung confetti at a concert,
perfumed laundry with a fresher smell than soap,

granted us a friendly earthquake where we're assured
they never happen, ribboned ordinary errands
into brilliance through the days.
That was the year you and I descended
into earth's mouth to her heart but rose again
to fly above her body, spread for us in schist, crag,
translucent minarets of rock, in piñon pine,
in scrims of mist and in pre-winter swirls of hail,
snowstorm rainbows lacing the aspen
still sunstruck, quivering, of our spines.
If that was an autumn, oh, we were driven
and drove ourselves into and beyond
a desert convinced of summer—giant saguaro, clusters
of brittlebush in brazen citrine bloom, the cactus-wren
warbling our names, and a cathedral of shale ridges
radiating twilight to the mulberry sky. The sun
specifically rose for us, fire-ruby singeing
your profile through the shadows as if it were
earth's birthday, as if something still
were giving birth, as if the indefatigable river
which had cut her way through rock for eons
were not for the first time now diverted, dammed,
as if the current could still reach the sea, the word
could still be spoken,
as if

And winter we have had. The winter
of our missed content—icebound arrivals,
the slink of spiral downswept in a double-arched
descent across snowdust, laughter in the teeth
of tears before a dying fire
and the word for the first time now

stopped at the lips
the word for the first time
dammed and diverted
the word not
flowing to the slickened sea.

Winter we have had, my love.
And autumns. And mostly springs.
But that full drowsily serene slow heat
of summer, the ripeness
that bursts the fruited skin and glows
through molten flesh, the lavish
lusty harvesting of dreams,
damp velvet midnight winds
and saltsweat dewey golden nakedness
at dawn, no, never, my love.
Summer we never had but once—
and that the first, the only, and the last.

And so, my dear,
    shall I compare thee to a springtime day?
    Thou art more brief, green, promising, and cruel.
    Shall I compare thee to an autumn day?
    Thou art more amber and more fugitive.
    Shall I compare thee to a winter day?
    Thou art more crisp, more bracing, and more infinite.
    Shall I compare thee to the summer day
we never had; that week high on far north foreign hills
where darkness never fell,
where light would have refracted love
through each night's phosphorescence
like a prism;

where the wise fjords listened for us,
almost paused,
but hearing nothing, flowed on,
stately, solemn,
that first last only summer
to the seasonless, stoic sea.

Daily Use

Tell me again how the persimmon wreath of flame
a live volcano weaves itself is rare
as poetry, how passion is a rupture
of reality—somewhat excessive, extreme
as spasms of laughter, a stroke
of luck perhaps, astonishing, a visitation—
but not for daily use.

Tell me again how certain shades, like larkspur,
wring the heart, how certain strains of music sting
beyond endurance, how one can never know Antarctica,
how silence is more nourishing than song,
how sanity prescribes we swallow the familiar,
cling, clasp, contrive, and compartmentalize—
for daily use.

Tell me again how this is not a failure
of nerve conspiring soberly with weariness to whisper
death as the grand style of living, a desire for peace
confused with safety. Insist instead how it is merely
different, another path, a health I do not comprehend.
Tell me to be fair, how air at certain heights is not for breathing—
for daily use.

Tell me how pleasant a nostalgic twinge can be
and more convenient by far than grief,
how fate precludes, how love deludes, how wood is wood,
stone stone, life real, how yesterday is unrelated
to tomorrow. Tell me how lovers pale into the best
of friends, how eagles can compact to pigeons—
for daily use.

/ / /

Tell me how no one, clearly, keeps in sight a comet.
Tell me again the sensible clichés: how muscles
heal by moving but the brain by rest; how permanence
spells depth but all things change; how no one really knows;
how passionate strangers flare in the night
all the more sweetly because they are doomed—
not for daily use.

I tell you I shall be a stranger
to no living thing.
I tell you the brain is a muscle,
that a comet keeps itself perpetually in sight.
I tell you everybody really knows.
I tell you friends are lost in the translation.
I tell you there are no discrete compartments—
for daily use.

I tell you wood, stone, cells, air whirl
with meson, pison, quark.
I tell you energy bends time and space
to its own will.
I tell you there are cliff-hung aeries beyond
all categories, where the wind's white singing
builds its nests—
for daily use.

I tell you not an instant passes
when the earth's core fails to boil
its common lava poems in preparation, I tell you that
reality is one long steady rupture,
a fatal laughter—
for daily use.

/ / /

Tell me again you know these things and more.
I tell you knowledge is not wisdom,
that you will have your silence,
that you have missed the meaning.

Tell me a final time that there is one
experience but many meanings.
I tell you there are multitudinous experiences
but, after all, one meaning.

I wish you yours, but take mine with me as I go,
to wheel wide-winged in thinner air
in search of my own kind, spilling
my lavish larkspur song on every second with a passion
for daily use.

Ten Sonnets to the Light Lady

I. *INVOCATION*

Not to be foolish, but a holy fool;
not to be mere beloved, but be lover;
not the exception that proves the rule,
not to provoke mild blushes but be fever.
Not to be flint or fuel but the flaming,
not grant permission but set free the act,
not to be lies or silence but the naming,
not to be approximate: exact.
Not to forget what dare not be remembered,
not to delude, despise, desert, despair;
not to enforce what cannot be engendered,
not to not trust, risk, dare, desire.
Fool I was, yes: exception, utterance, flame,
not to have known that I was what I wished to become.

II. FLYING SOUTH

Mourning another season given over,
we seek an opposite spring, a hemisphere
in thaw, new favorite of our fickle heat.
Few have the stamina to complete the flight.
Most weary, mate, and nest along the way
—an equatorial peace—or, braver, fly
toward plumage-raucous lust in tropic sun.
Rarely does one winged animal press on,
air-obsessed, driven, sleet-scaled, across a sea
indifferent under alien stars. That one, they say,
has overshot the south. Yet to a salt-scoured
eye like hers, the crystal polar dunes' wild
upward rush to clasp her fall must gleam
luminous as a remembered dream,
          past song, fear, gravity, past death, past shattered form.

III. BOSCHE COUNTRY

> "I am in Bosch country . . . If the words come, the
> reality will afterwards?"
>   —Doris Lessing, *The Four Gated City*

Nothing is questioned? Then no reply is wise.
Nothing is answered? Then nothing can be asked.
Nothing is cursed or blessed? no paradise
is scalable? no purgatory's risked?
When nothing's utterable, why, nothing dies
by that. Or lives. Stick figures can refrain
indefinitely gesturing disguise
upon a silent, flat, bland, temporal terrain.
But let a single voice articulate
one word's rude scarlet against such pastels,
and all those secular mimes gesticulate
in exile to a hundred sundry hells.
So I, undamned to my damnation, do confess
my unasked question to your answer answerless.

IV. BRAILLE

Blind, illiterate longing strains my vision
through the edge of fingertip antennae
scanning your every code, smile, tear, wound, lesion:
this is the way you unfold, struck-winged, free;
there, that's the muscle spasming in fear;
these are the lines of mourning, those of laughter;
here is the birthmark, yes, and there the scar,
the lips that will not speak to me till after
it is too late, you think, and safe. Dark
are the ways I read you, patient, at the bone,
to bless the core of you that will not break
and recognize what bleeds there to be known.
In search of what you see, at last I find
your eyes. My god, my love! You too are blind.

V.   BALEFIRE

Greensilver sapling, her body—a juniper
where nest enshadowed descant creatures of her soul—
stiffens toward me ever in desire.
Then eyes, lips, palms, spine, senses all
spring to encircle her, strip her songstruck limbs
like druids at the solstice, celebrants
assembled chanting in a shade who dooms
herself, glad-spread, to wanton reverence.
Gone now those greygreen berries used to cure
and kill, that tonic resin pungency.
Starved, ragged, her devout crouch through winter
in ritual cells. Mute, they no longer pray.
But nightly each creeps forth and, suffering, learns
her timbre at the hearth of me still burns.

VI.   FALCON AND FALCONER

Only the female is fit for falconry,
and only a few: swift, pitiless, compact,
so gentle that her indecisive prey
dies embraced while soaring, unmangled, perfect.
Immaculate fledgling, fierce, precise she trains
under the eye of the falconer whose own skill
is half of the mutual mastery. One learns
how to kill cleanly and return. The other's guile
studies how to teach her, let her go, and watch.
Which of us dare call first, then, "Peregrine love, you
shall not stay blinded, bound, once this my touch
unhoods you to dawnburst, winglift, blood-sequined snow,
yourself"? Nor shall I stir until we've guessed
whose talons, yours or mine, light upon whose wrist.

VII. DREAMING THE VOLCANO

Barefoot on steaming ash I climbed toward you,
unhurried, unscorched: this was our element.
Behind me, sudden cinquefoil slate blue
lupine sprang and flowered in each footprint.
We had been warned, you and I, about this place:
volatile, steep, erupting ancient geysers,
sulfurine, fountaining fiery lace.
The scarp itself was sintered with dead lovers.
But we met as always at the appointed crater,
laughing, eyes blazing as we leapt the crust,
twin plumes of lava coursing through each other,
to arc, flame, flow in sacred lust.
Then, safe in your smoldering arms, I slept,
at peace. And woke in bed, alone. And wept.

VIII. INTENSIVE CARE

Stand back, my heart, think, look alive.
The brain can be mad or dying, the body too:
wounds stuttering muscle through a nerveless glove
of skin too slack or seared or scarred to show
clots unfestering in arteries undammed—
the whole great undiscovered continent laid waste,
blind, speechless, deaf, aware. Undimmed
until the final wire is cut, persist.
Stand back from all the rest and suffer clearly.
Not in the ivory skulltower dares memory breathe
nor there the fool reside, however holy,
but here—this furnace where you implode and seethe.
Endure a while, my heart. Then hemorrhage free
my sanguine rapids wildward to no sea.

IX.   A NOCTURNAL UPON ST. LUCY'S DAY

(with obeisance to John Donne)

The midnight of my year is your year's noon,
your summer by my wintering grows weathered.
It flares too late for me, for you too soon,
this constellation: the Goat cannot be tethered.
My climate weeps above your seasoned drought,
a wheel of difference on a hub of Same
reversing us when either risks the doubt
that neither our age nor ages are to blame.
Should my life's late noon scorch, in time, your midnight
as now your darkness blazes down my day,
permit no tears to blur the final sight
of how we dared not rush, dared not delay.
Outlive me, love. You too at last will sing
"Dead, yet am I every living thing."

X. THE HUNGRY WILL

There crouches caged in me a hungry will
that never lets me rest but eats my hours,
swallows whole serenity, devours
my sleep, and is most famished when most full.
Pacing, it roars, gnaws, ravenous with lack.
It craves raw limits beyond appetite,
consuming morseled patience with one bite,
tasting bland compromise to spit it back.
No tepid act can feed it, no tidbit love,
no rationed liberty, no candied lie,
no mince of truth however savory.
It wants a wilder prey, or else to starve.
Meat, sinew, blood, its only nourishment is me,
and it awaits my dying, to range satiate and free.

Going to the Wars

(after Richard Lovelace)

Tell me not, Sweet, I am despotic
      that from the vagary
of your silk breasts and brain erotic
      to war and poems I fly.

True, a new lover now I chase,
      the last foe in the field,
and with a wilder lust embrace
      the age and pen I wield.

Such frailty may prove a mettle
      you refuse to guess:
I cannot love you just a little
      without loving living less.

Damn You, Lady
(THE FUNKY DOUBLE SONNET TRAGICOMIC
LESBIAN FEMINIST BLUES)

Damn you, lady, get out of my blood for good.
Your eyes, hair, laugh, your politics—erase
them—how your body's swift lewd grace once stood
beside me, how love lit your falcon face.

> Damn you, lady, I refuse to wail
> one moment longer so uncritically
> over you—as if I were a fool
> (or even incorrect politically).

Your gestures in quickliquid flow,
your voice, indigo as a violin's—
get out. Go, let my dreams sleep free
of you, your fragrance, words, songs, silences . . .

> Lovesick morons fail the revolution,
> mooning about while work needs to be done,
> and feminism's surely the solution
> to everything—except your being gone.

. . . the way you slept, woke, moved at midnight,
your antic grin that struck and blazed me glad
to be alive, the way you loved a fight
in a just cause. The way you drove me mad.

> Damn you, lady, I will not obsess
> one second more. Love's just a masquerade
> at which we women, like men, can oppress
> (an awkward truth we'd rather not parade).

/ / /

But see? I have regained myself entire,
immune to you, asbestos to your fire.

Damn you, lady, I will yet live through
this memory, everywhere I turn, of you.

Even at This Hour

Surely I have loved you well enough
that even at this hour
something of me in you can recognize
how your heart, yours, beats
its tattoo through my body,
how all my curses and my incantations
are as if keened by a sybil towering
on her stone of prophecy, wrists
bent as though broken, head exposed
above a cauldron cold as the waiting
for god's utterance.

Surely you have loved me well enough
that even in this space
something of you in me can recognize
how naked beneath her pythian robe there sways
a woman marked forever by her calling
but still human, who even now
would with her own nails tear apart
linen, breast, and prison bars of rib
to pluck this heart of you,
raw living garnet, from the cage
it is not in me to become.

Surely you and I have loved enough
to recognize that even at this hour
she would seize it in both hands and hold it
high, still pulsing, to the higher pulse of moon,
then place it as an offering purified of hope—
if in response the essence of you
might, a vapor, issue
from the cleft rock's fissure

to spiral out, float free,
and seem to
disappear.

Famine

This must stop.
I must stop writing you
these messages, stop
leaking love from these cracked
vessels of poems. I must
stop this gathering of memory's
brittle twigs, searching them out
at dawn, at sundown, bundling them
together, hauling them with me
everywhere as if such kindling
could warm me through the densifying night.

This must stop, this wading hip-deep
through leeches in mudwater days
as if to sow a hardier strain of rice
for future sustenance. I must censor
these thoughts, strangle this longing, cease
this squatting in the merciless sun,
this waiting to no purpose, this
scouring of recollection,
this rasping of detail
against the mortar of reality.
Surely you see why this must stop.

Somewhere a woman needs us.
Somewhere a woman is hauling fetid water
up a hill, the yoke across her back
bearing down toward bone the way
your lightest touch did, her cracked
vessels leaking the burden
onto a steep trail, spotting the dust,
but she is a woman who has no other vessel

and she is thirsty
and this must stop.

Somewhere a woman is gathering branches,
sorting the twigs not already rotted,
seeking the dry ones which might yet flare
into a bluetipped tawny leap of flame
the way your slightest glance did.
Her fingers splinter with the finding
but she is a woman who has no other fuel
and she is cold
and this must stop.

Somewhere a woman is planting rice,
planting sorghum, beans, cassava, corn,
somewhere she stoops shuffles stoops
again along the rows she works,
the back of her head her shoulders spine
braising in the midday heat, her haunches
one forked ache. She must
believe that what she tenders
the acidic rocky soil or the leech-thick
swamp will root, grow, flower, fruit
the way I once believed
two women such as you and I—
no, this must stop. But she is
educated for no other labor,
a woman occupied beyond survival
with a belief beyond survival
and this must stop.

Somewhere a woman is grinding meal

between two stones, the same way love
is ground to powder between two human hearts,
the way love husks and pulverizes, winnows
those who really handle it, somewhere
she pounds, chafes, sifts it with the weight
of her whole kneeling body, arms cramped
with pressure of what she cannot grasp
the way space weights the shape of you
in my embrace of vacancy. She does this
every day, it takes too long, it yields her
insufficiency, the stone is worn
smooth as her soul with pounding but she is
a woman who knows no other means of nourishment
and she is hungry
and this must stop.

Somewhere a woman I have loved
still writes to me that she must stop
sending me these messages let go
strangle them release herself avert her eyes.
Somewhere the woman you are
once told yourself that this must stop,
that you must send no further messages like these
into the silence of yet another woman.
Somewhere each of these women has vowed to each:
*My love, I will not fail you: never
censor yourself with me.* And somewhere each
has turned her face away, hand to the lips, hush,
and we are women who know no other life
but longing, no other death but famine,
and this must stop.

/ / /

"Love is more complex than theory"
I wrote once: "There is no
pure act possible." Must I now
write that loss is more complex than theory,
there is no loving possible? Re-learn from women
what I was forced to learn from men?
Turn my face away from seeing
dry-eyed how the woman wields
the blade of clitoridectomy,
the woman weaves and winds the cloth
to bind the foot, the woman veils herself
and veils her daughter, the woman
drowns the female infant, fires her maid
for stealing food, burns her son's wife
in a dowry murder, beats her child as she
herself was beaten, looks in the other direction
when her husband slides his hand between
their daughter's legs? See how the woman
smiles and lies, the woman is afraid, the woman
betrays the woman and then weeps, says this
must stop but then persists, see how the woman
can risk only so much before she comes to hate
the challenge, how the woman turns her face away,
turns from her mother, daughter, sister,
from her woman lover, from the woman
who writes these things because I have no other
vessel, no other fuel, no other means but this
and this must stop?

How do I stop, then?
How do I shade the back of my brain
from this baking? How do I cease writing you,

translate these messages into a strangled civility,
quit following the trail of your passing,
spotting your dust with blood leaked
from the vessels of my pen and veins?
How do I stop gathering dead wood of what once
put forth leaves in a spring lime-green with desire?
How do I learn to see as separate
all these patterns of misshapen suffering—
as if love were not food and water,
as if love were not fire's light and heat,
as if love were not marks on a page, uneffaced,
as if love were not fragile and sharp as a shoot
up-puncturing soil and greenly entering the air?
How do I stop naming love as a thirst, a hunger,
a chill, a labor, a complex pure act?
Stop knowing all famine, cold, weariness,
lies, tears, betrayals, fear, turnings away, all
as the thwarting of love? How do I stop,
learn to unread and unwrite, censor, veil, bind, burn,
grind, winnow myself, learn to drown
in the silence being readied for me, smile
lies within it? How do I halt, let the vessel
drop, break, the embers wink out, the soil
run fallow, the grain drift where it will?
How do I slice out my sex how
hack out my tongue?

I must
cease this daily invisible labor of loving
to no purpose but staying alive for no purpose
but daily invisible labor must stop
you have tried to listen, hear, warn me

of this, you have learned how and wanted
to teach me but she is a woman I am and we know
this way only
how do I learn to give up
what I now know I never
had and will not

                              how do I speak to you through
smiles and lies

                              how understand
this daily invisible suffering
     will   go   on   how can I
begin again stoop rise again

                              conjugate need
and shuffle begin to
    stop hush avert your eyes

                              a woman needs
how
do I categorize the intolerable

                              I need, you

        how
        do
        I

                              need, she
    quantify hunger,

                              needs, we need, they
unrecognize thirst as all thirsts
      how
undefine chill as the absence of warmth,
disrelate power from powerlessness, dis-
connect loving you to no purpose
from the common, acceptable lovelessness
civilly starving some woman somewhere?

                   / / /

Deny this denial, betray these betrayals *how*
do I stop without learning the ways
      that a woman stops somewhere and
            dies
from this hunger, thirst, cold, from exhaustion,
from someone turning away, dying for
            lack
      of the means to put marks on paper
      so as to remember so as to send messages
            lack
      of the voice to speak what she feels
      across smiles, lies, tears, silence,
            lack
      of the knowledge, the means, how to
stop
      the arms cramping around no embrace
stop
      the ache in the body that knows how
      to stop just before numbness but then
      to begin again
stop
      the throat parched for naming
            how
      do I fill this hunger
      to love you as if
      such a freedom
      could feed the whole world?

I must stop writing you such messages
as these, you have tried to make me see why
I must stop surely

                                 the cry in the throat

there are other messages I must study
you have tried to teach me smiles lies no
tears there is no pure loss possible

                                              strangled in the throat

        how can I
when to stop is more complex than theory,
when there is no pure end possible?
        Still I must   let it go
        strangle it   hush, turn away
             the face go veiled
    cease   finish it   quit
        must I
refuse this trying to understand *refuse*
this certainty that somewhere
        right at this moment a woman
because she must give birth again

                                    the cry in the throat

    or because she tries to stop

                                        strangle it

giving birth again or because
    she tries to stop again

                              writing you these messages

    because she tries to stop
hush avert your eyes
    at this moment somewhere
    a woman is dying

    and this must

Giving Up the Ghost

Giving up the ghost is simple:
an involuntary act forced on you
as by the bullet's plunge
through lung, the wash of lightning
that shudders the brain bright blank,
the voice you love, weeping
through the telephone,
telling the truth at last.

But you must live
an afterlife of dying.
With what do you inhale, now
that the knifeblade's slow withdrawal
trailed your last breath out behind it?
You move calmly. You hang up the phone.
You listen. Silence swells the room
to an intolerable space. No tears come.
Your hands lie still in your lap.
You try, but you cannot imagine
any terror that could make them tremble now.

Giving up the ghost seems simple.
You have yet to beggar yourself
in spendthrift mourning, yet to learn
a lust for sleep greater even than for her,
yet to dream and wake again into remembering,
yet to stalk the winter floor at midnight
yourself a ghost, trying to understand,
calculating ancient errors you must have made,
feeling a fool, wanting to be fair,
philosophizing love as an illusion.

/ / /

You have yet to lose yourself utterly
struck down by a particular piece of music,
yet to find yourself wounded
by commonplace, lethal things:
A hand-knit sweater the shade of heather at dusk.
A grainwhorled wooden bowl. A curve
of pottery splashed with the birth
of a constellation in its nightsky glaze.
Flyleaf inscriptions in too many books
for safety.

Giving up the ghost seemed simple.
As if the choice were anger
at the woman you love
or at the woman you are.
As if she were mere metaphor
for a poem: her body, a branch
of flowering quince; her brain,
quicksilver mercury; her spirit,
a lucifer hummingbird in mid-air shimmer.
As if she were mere subject matter.
But she was never subject.
And she mattered.

Little by little, without promise
or warning, the inanimate weapons
will give up her ghost, return to being
gifts a lover gave you once.
Little by little, music will stab
your senses by being simply music,
the night hours pleat back between
crisp sweeps of daylight rustle.

/ / /

Little by little, your poems
will write you other images.

Giving up the ghost will then be simple
as discovering you have slept,
can work, recall an appetite for laughter.
What you will not anticipate
is that this resurrection will ravish you
as murder, this health taste
like voluntary dying, shudder you
sudden into bright blank fear,
suffer through you as an ultimate betrayal:
offal, bloody in the abattoir of the heart.

Crueler than the loss of love, the surrendering
of loss. Worse than the disease,
the affliction of its healing.
Lazaran, you shriek against the final
torture: miracle.
Yet it will rack you into life again,
pitiless, indifferent to the false confession
you babble, extracting the secret you clasp
in futile loyalty. This is the dying
afterdeath, the revisionism of desire. This is
giving up the grief.

Pray at this moment, pray
as if you still possessed a soul, pray
that the telephone does not ring.

Relativity

"One may say the eternal mystery of the world
is its comprehensibility."
—Albert Einstein

Light-years can pass, and dark, and still the speed
            accelerates.
Distance extends between us: we are lost,
            encompassed still.
Suns nova, stars implode, particles spin, stream, blur,
            moons wax and wane:
no matter the expanse of our removal
            we remain.
No matter the vacuum, no matter the entropy,
            our energy.
Sundered, remote, at farthest reach we poise
            circumferenced
no matter the lengths we range to fly our own
            immensity.
No matter how far it stretches us, we reach
            toward one another.
No matter whose maps, paths, territories:
            the encounter.
No matter how ultimate the span, our space
            the intimate.
No matter the acedia, this helpless
            celebration.
Intelligence has seized us, though we struggle,
            for its own,
this mystery simple as a quantum thought's
            design made plain:
You and I dwell in different hemispheres
            of a single brain.

Syzygy

All day today
I have been sweeping death—
diary leaves of summer,
drifts of crisp skin—
some to burn, some to save,
compost against inevitable snows,
as if spring could be invented.
All day today
wading in brittle burgundy, dustgold
tangerine, black-veined brass curls,
I envied such a death:
so gaudy, so useful, and so natural.

All night tonight
I have been sorting papers—
artifacts of the deciduous year
deceptively simple as black on white—
some to burn, some to save,
testament against silence,
merciful forgetting, indifference.
All night tonight
sifting and resorting certain scraps
I cannot burn and dare not save and
so invent to some use here:
an exorcism, an alchemy, a transliteration.

    One reads:
    Time out of joint again,
    no space for passion
    in this shrunken century.

/ / /

Another reads:
the candlewick nods—wild hoopoe,
its flame comb snapping behind; an old
unlit candle put to blaze at last
so that a woman's shadow
can emerge in profile
defined against it.

        Still another reads:
        the pathology,
        the phenomenology,
        the ontology
        of loving.

If that were all, I could rest
now. Gaudy, useful, natural.
But there are others:

        Wild rice and orchids,
        physics and chicken soup.

Eagles never perch by balance.
Eagles perch facing into the wind.
Eagles perch by leaning against the wind
for balance.
Eagles sleep this way.

I am
in debt
in love
in doubt
in danger.

            / / /

If this were all, I could invent
some use to turn it to. Exorcism,
alchemy, transliteration.
But there are others:

       Icons everywhere I go.

   Elephants wave branches at the moon
   with what an observer might infer
   is superstitious reverence.

          The blinding wheatsheen of her breasts.
Some are penned
by my own hand. Some
are printed, clipped, torn.
Some are in a language I fear
I understand, drawn in spirals of red
ochre on greenstone jade:

     This is the resting place of the god.
     Take counsel: carry a godstick for balance.

        Lacking any surface at all,
        the planet Uranus continues
        to radiate intense heat from its core.

   A place of infinite trust
   and resurrection.

Some are bound
in notebooks. Others
may be freesia petals,
slivers of flint, a strand of wool

the color of new berries,
a sheet of rice paper frayed
as the moon tonight:

>   Where is the other side
>   of the fire?

> An extinct species might cry out,
> Death is one thing, an end
> to birth is something else.

>   Black ice is a term
>   for the fine, almost invisible mist
>   which can form a treacherous coating,
>   then build upon itself. Black ice
>   can rise on land or sea,
>   phenomenon of winter
>   coastlines.

All week this week
a rare alignment
of sun, moon, and earth, results
in greater gravitational pull worldwide.
This is called syzygy.
The moon, as well, is now
at closest distance to the earth, in perigee.
Global high tides, storms, flooding,
wind sudden from directions unexpected:

>   She wears the practiced smile
>   of a woman who desires you
>   to perceive both her suffering
>   and her efforts to conceal it.

/ / /

Maps of the earth's core
show not a smooth sphere
but a landscape with mountains
taller than Everest, canyons
six times deeper than the Grand Canyon.
This was discovered through seismic
tomography, a technique
similar to a cat-scan on the brain.

Notes for a chameleon poem:
prehensile tail, laterally
compressed body, independent
movable eyes, tongue as long
as its spine, name means lion-
on-the-ground, an old world lizard.

All month this month
I have almost thought:
some are penned, bound.
Some drift, dare not be saved.
Some cannot burn, are clipped, torn.
If that were all, I could sleep
now. A gaudy alchemy, a natural transliteration:

When a white whale-calf dies,   Apples,
the mother tries to support its body   coffee,
at the surface in life-giving air,   and kisses.
sometimes for many days.
When she finally loses the calf,   How did Venus become
she may adopt a stone or chunk of wood   a planet
as surrogate.   so hot and desolate?

                                         / / /

All year this year
I have been sweeping death,
sorting papers, inventing counsel:
Soon, it is coming, it will start to form,
then build upon itself, deceptively simple.
Prepare. Do not mistake it
as debt, love, doubt, or danger.

Lifelong this life
I have almost thought:
Strip the deciduous self down
still further, prune, pare, cut
deeper to the core, peel yourself,
cast it away. You will have no need
to burn or save or understand
once the other begins.

All day tonight
scanning its approach, now,
sooner than expected: a blinding,
an icon lacking any surface
it approaches, too late now for alchemy or envy
as I fray, blaze, sink beneath it, nodding
while it wades through me
sifting extinct skins cast by a woman's shadow,
unmistakably
light as a stone surrogate for mourning,
this gravitational spiral,
this roar of flooding,
this seismic dispassion, this touch
natural and desolate as the kiss of a lizard—
a scent like snow in the air now,

a rare
alignment:

Show me the unexpected   direction from which

the wind comes sudden

that I may face into it,
lean against its rising,
and sleep this way.

Poetry in an Old Key

"I believe that in this physical, space-time world of our experi-
ence there are things which do not fit the grammatical
scheme of expression. But they are not necessarily blind,
inconceivable, mystical affairs; they are simply matters
which require to be conceived through some symbolistic
schema other than discursive language."
—Susanne K. Langer

Why, caring as I do for trees,
am I condemned to poetry? why compelled
to serve a life sentence stuttering this
syntax of desire, each poem straining
to manifest the inexpressible on paper,
a ritual offering, a superstition, a power,
prayer, seduction, clue, risk, awe, act,
as if my life depended on it?

The Aztecs knew paper as a sacred substance;
conquered towns sent millions of rolls each year
as tribute to the capital. It was not wasted
on words. Shamans painted images and soaked
the sheets with blood, provoking their divinities
to action. Under the Conquistadores, papermaking
was illegal: possession of paper was sufficient grounds
for the charge of idolatry, a sentence to be burned.

An artist (the philosopher reasons)
seeks not to arouse or convey feeling
but to portray what she knows about the nature
of feeling; once in possession of rich
symbolism, that knowledge may exceed her
whole experience. Genius (the artist shrugs
in answer) manifests itself
through attention to detail.

/ / /

Today, sorcerers among the Nahua and Otomís
still paint paper spirits, cut paper god-dolls,
fold paper to trap ghosts, string paper infants
on the clothesline to ease childbirth, plant paper
to help crops grow, burn paper to dispel the winds
of evil, decorate paper with the drippings
of live sacrifice—the collective soul that reinvents
the universe through individual acts of superstition.

It would be best to recognize oneself as they do:
an idolator hunched spelling over blood-soaked paper,
a shaman working toward health or madness,
a vehicle for words recycled on recycled pages,
a knowledge beyond its own experience,
a symbol of itself, an image of a poet
forming in the reader's mind, or a Scheherazade, telling
story after story, just to stay alive.

The Found Season

Certain farm mornings
can make one believe Atlantis
has been regained, surfacing
serenely from the depths of loss,
artless as a mist-wrapped dawn
ribboned with rosella song.
Hot tea, fresh milk;
the radio news, buffered by distance;
the telephone news, muffled by distance.

Two women, four hands, one garden (many weeds).
Hoe scrape and spade-clang a carillon.
I have been staking tomatoes: you claim
my hair smells of tomato flowers.
You have been mending fences: I claim
you are amazonian, the freckles
tooled on your plum-colored shoulders
small gold stars on red leather armor.
We play these hours hard, intent as children
on a carousel—up, down, around,
astride mythical doe unicorns
who wink at us through white-lashed amber eyes.

There is no time for brooding,
and psychologies have less centrality
once the Canada geese bestow
their residence on the pond.
Gathering blackberries in a sudden summer rain,
we peel free of our soaked thin shirts,
our fingertips stained mauve. Later,
we set homemade jam and homemade poetry.
No worlds are shaken. Such days,

transparent, are the finest
life can offer: fastidiously uneventful.

Dusk brightens into evening
with a bonfire streaming sparks
the way a brain streams thought, celebrating
its own conflagration, flinging its heat
at the firmament. Circling the blaze, I think:
this is the other side of the fire,
where starlight eclipses grief and disbelief,
where even the patterns of ash rise gracefully.

After, we walk homeward up the hill, desire
matching our strides to hers, entering
us, coursing moon-marrow through the bone.
The old-fashioned claw-footed bathtub
is large enough for two.
Our laughter is a sweet, a still-warm jam
shared as it melts, like understanding.
I am drunk with it, babbling:
carillon, carousel, caritas, carry us,
carry oh carry us on.

> Having used up all my words
> to invoke the reality,
> I had none left to describe it.
> This was perhaps the moment
> for which you had been waiting:
> a stillness flowing over stones
> so smoothly one would not suspect
> —except for what quickened, fire-opal, in your glance—

that in such silence we could ride
wild white water, cataracting
to the open sea.

Arbitrary Bread

> "All poems are made by one poet, a woman poet."
> —Marina Tsvetaeva

Learning as if for the first time how
to make poetry.
No additives, no processed flours:
only whole grains, salt, honey, yeast.
I have kneaded shadows
and watched them rise, swallowed them,
fed them to others, too long,
fighting to cheat starvation.

> When the last rat was devoured
> in the refugee camp of Rashidiyeh,
> the men petitioned the mullahs
> for religious dispensation
> to permit the eating of human flesh.
> No one asked who would cook it.

> The already unclean ones whose lives
> were dumb clay, they
> would cook it, know how
> to spice it, disguise it,
> lie as they served it,
> so as not to disgust sons, fathers,
> brothers, and husbands: the raw flesh
> they had birthed, suckled,
> cooked, and still fed.

Still trying to learn
how to make sense of it,
where is the boiling point,
what degree heat melts the crystal,
at what precise moment
the nerves sing recognition.

/ / /

A lifetime spent learning
how to spice it, disguise it, lie
as I serve it: this dumb clay, this raw flesh
that is me.

> Men make impressions, arbitrary decisions, names
> for themselves, wars, profits, laws, reputations,
> deals, fortunes, threats, enemies, promises, tracks.
>
> Women make do, ends meet, babies, way, clothing,
> breakfast and dinner and supper, quilts, homes,
> apologies, baskets, beds, light of it, room.

Beginning again, unlearning how
to make jokes, compromises and bargains,
the best of it. Relearning how
to make trouble, a living, a practice of politics.
Cracking wheat, crushing millet, dissolving
salt crystals, pounding the dough. Waiting
the first rise. Reshaping the dough. Waiting
the second. Heating the oven of metal or clay.

> Winnie Mandela stands outside
> the smoking timbers of what yesterday
> was her home. She stares. She does not enter.
> Lost articles—inanimate speechless things—flare
> to mind, each vivid, crisped, with grief.
> The books. The diaries. The humble gifts
> from ordinary people. The wedding pictures.
> The letters, thirty years of them, from him
> in prison. While she raised the children,
> carried messages, was banned, was under house arrest,

in jail and out again, while she made visits
to him, made speeches, made an example
of herself, was made his symbol, was made
a metaphor for freedom. Men manage to make
their revolutions from abstraction. But no slogans
can be made from the thoughts of a woman
sifting the ashes of her life.
The last bed in which they ever slept together,
gone now. The baby pictures. The headscarf her mother
left her, the recipes. The saved invitations
to far countries where she could not go.
The mirror she aged in.

Over and over, practicing how
to make a fresh start, making the most of knowing
the worst of it—not what's assumed:
that they can torture, degrade, kill, erase you,
but this—that they can just tire you out.
My son, grown now, sits making
his music, pressing all the right keys,
his darkening hair tarnished by late summer light.
He is the last man
I will forgive.
Again, every woman surveying
the state of her life as again it withers away,
searching the ashes for something, finding
an edge of it, tugging, trying to free
the shredded banner of her red worker heart.

Marion Todd, of Fairbury, Nebraska, was shy.
She never thought of breaking the law.
"One day," she said, "I was suddenly hit

with an image of a nuclear train being blocked
by a pile of wheat—a grain that sustains life."
So, holding a handful of wheat, she sat down
on the tracks and waited for hours in February snow,
until the train carrying nuclear missiles
bore down on her, until it finally
screamed to a stop two feet away, until
they called the police, until she was dragged
off, charged, and jailed—still shy.

Again and again learning how
to make peace:
cracking open the whole grain of anger,
crushing the fear, dissolving the sense
of futility, deliberately making
believe,
pounding, shaping, reshaping the act—
arbitrary but this time our own.
One woman demands *bread and roses.* Another invokes
bread, blood, poetry. In Chile, the women say bread
in the face of God. Feeding each other
the honey and salt of it, learning to make
the connections.

Clay is the wild crystal
making itself through eons of weathering
by the pounding, cracking, crushing of rocks,
the dissolving of rocks, the absorption
of water in minuscule pores, developing "defects"
in crystalline lattices which collect energy, store it,
transmit it. This is one definition
of a life form.

/ / /

A regular crystal is perfect, blank until
it receives an imposed pattern of charges.
                    But clay replicates, layering
pattern on pattern of ions coded in flaws.
Disorder, the woman scientist whispers,
is precisely the thing which can hold information.
Strike an ordinary lump of clay with a hammer:
it blows ultraviolet energy for a month.

Learning as if for the first time how
to make merry:
woman to woman, eye to wide open eye—
a choice arbitrary
as my own will, my flesh undisguised,
no longer young but no longer helpless.
Rare only in how I express this, our shared
commonality, I am wild clay
whose nerves sing recognition, blow energy, store
information, transmit these messages
in willful, flawed code
to a woman, a sister, a lover
who rises like yeast, like a poem, raw
in my hand, teaching me now
as if for the first time how
to make love.

                    I want to make
                    this so plain
                    that every woman can feed herself with it,
                    make it her own, make it
                    mean what she chooses, make
                    demands of it, make

it available, make
mischief, a difference, a miracle, ready.
I want to say this in the quietest voice possible:

> *Give us this day*
> *our arbitrary bread.*

Do I make myself
clear?

Upstairs in the Garden

Nothing is ever quite where you
expected it to be. The other
glove, a radio news bulletin,
coriander on the spice shelf, this
poem, making its way unannounced.

Something is always sharper or smaller,
larger or duller, sooner
or later—yourself, for example,
at any given moment older than you
had anticipated. Yet here you are, hurtling

toward your galaxy's edge, a character
in a poem, nebulas underfoot and overhead,
north spinning below south if viewed
from, say, Andromeda. The top of anything
is just the base for something else, to

wit: the garden on my ceiling
three stories in the air above a city
street, its feathery Japanese red maple
unruffled at being out of place.
Visitors comment politely on the view,

meaning other buildings. I watch instead
a wildness that at once is everywhere
and patient: how the indigo clematis, fragile-
fingered, pries apart the chimney bricks;
how cutter bees work, making lace from rose leaves.

Once, I thought myself a city woman, safe
amidst electric intersections, brain-child

ministered to by body-servant. Imagine how
surprised mind was to find that matter
minded, mattered, and materialized where least

expected—as brain itself, or as a garden
I once called mine before I understood just who
owns who and who lives understairs in service.
Well, I have had worse employment than this
deadheading daisies, pruning wisteria vines,

studying seed packets, hosing soot
from the tomatoes. One autumn, overwarm,
brought daffodils and freesia. One summer, toxic
air cottoned each noon with fungal haze. Nothing
is ever where you quite expected it to be.

Yet every spring I coax bean tendrils up
a trellis, shift pots of basil, sage, thyme,
tarragon, chives, rue, and rosemary
from windowsills to roof. I had not thought
to be this eccentric quite so soon.

But just as nothing is always where you didn't
plan it—the telephone call at four a.m.,
the lump in the breast, the envy shadowing
a friend's expression—so something is
also always where you barely dreamed it:

the gift of peaches ripening in a wicker basket,
a hummingbird poised, whirling color, at the feeder
you'd filled in a gesture to impossibility,

a particular face lit with love
to see you enter the room.

Making its way unannounced, eternity
suggests you practice it at any given moment.
So do I find myself sometimes
when least expected—at dawn perhaps
kneeling on the tar while finches help

me thin the carrots, or at dusk when lightning
bugs and streetlamps wink on together—
rehearsing how the bottom of anything is just
the top of something else. No
paradise this garden, but a homely act

of earthkeeping, mid-air yet rooted nonetheless
beneath white skies perforate with poison,
but beneath, as well, ancient stubborn energies
still constellating existence as a way of being
inappropriate and beautiful. Then, hesitating

in the doorway as night rises, I can smile at dirt
left crescenting my fingernails from weeding lettuces
or poems, breathe the last mint and honeysuckle, turn,
and descend up into darkness, practicing eternity,
to rest, while life grows on above my sleeping head.

Robin Morgan has published four books of poetry and seven books of prose. She is a recipient of the National Endowment for the Arts Grant Award in Poetry, and her poems have appeared widely in literary journals in the United States and abroad, and have been translated into Arabic, French, German, Greek, Italian, Japanese, Portuguese, Spanish, and Swedish. *Poetry* (Chicago) wrote of her work: "Robin Morgan will be regarded as one of our first-ranking poets."

Copyright Notices

Excerpt from *The Plague* by Albert Camus reprinted by permission of Alfred A. Knopf, Inc.

Excerpt from *A Passage to India* by E. M. Forster, copyright 1924 by Harcourt Brace Jovanovich, Inc. and renewed in 1952 by E. M. Forster, reprinted by permission of the publisher.

Excerpt from *The Four Gated City* by Doris Lessing reprinted by permission of Alfred A. Knopf, Inc.

Excerpt from *Dear Theo: The Autobiography of Vincent Van Gogh*, edited by Irving Stone, reprinted by permission of Doubleday, a division of Bantam, Doubleday, Dell Publishing Group, Inc.

Excerpt from "Late Hymn from the Myrrh Mountain" from *The Collected Poems of Wallace Stevens*, reprinted by permission of Alfred A. Knopf, Inc.

Index of Titles
and First Lines

INDEX

DATE DUE

GAYLORD			PRINTED IN U.S.A.